Unloved and Endangered Animals

What You Can Do

GREEN ISSUES IN FOCUS

Cindy Watson

Enslow Publishers, Inc.
40 Industrial Road
Box 398
Berkeley Heights, NJ 07922
USA
http://www.enslow.com

*To my wolf caller, Jade, whose incredible capacity to love
these misunderstood animals inspired this book.*

Acknowledgments

*Thanks to Sherri Somerville (aka Mary Lou George) for her constant
encouragement, unwavering support and rich friendship; Brian Henry
for kick-starting my writing career; Jade, Chase and Dakota for their
honest and enthusiastic feedback; and my husband, Don, for picking
up the extra slack to let me do what I do. Thanks too, to all those people
who fight every day to protect our misunderstood animals worldwide.*

Library of Congress Cataloging-in-Publication Data

Watson, Cindy.
    Unloved and endangered animals : what you can do / Cindy Watson.
       p. cm. — (Green issues in focus) Includes bibliographical references and index.
    Summary: "Discusses endangered animals throughout the world, including coral
      reef, bees, bats, marine turtles, wolves, sharks, and frogs and what can be done
      to help save them"—Provided by publisher.
    ISBN 978-0-7660-3345-0
    1. Endangered species—Juvenile literature. I. Title.
    QL83.W39 2010 591.68—dc22

                                                     2009001372

Printed in the United States of America

042010 Lake Book Manufacturing, Inc., Melrose Park, IL

10 9 8 7 6 5 4 3 2 1

♻ Enslow Publishers, Inc., is committed to printing our books on recycled paper. The
paper in every book contains 10% to 30% post-consumer waste (PCW). The cover board
on the outside of each book contains 100% PCW. Our goal is to do our part to help
young people and the environment too!

Illustration Credits: Copyright © Bigfoto (www.bigfoto.com), pp. 24, 32, 41, 118; Clipart
.com, p. 12; Library of Congress, p. 14; National Oceanic and Atmospheric Administra-
tion Photo Library, pp. 19, 28, 79, 108, 111, 117; Photos.com, pp. 12, 87, 91, 100, 102,
124; Shutterstock, pp. 3, 4, 38, 46, 48, 51, 53, 56, 83, 106, 117, 119, 120, 122, 123; U.S.
Fish and Wildlife Service, pp. 60, 63, 65, 70, 75, 114, 121, 125.

Cover Illustration: Photos.com.

Contents

1

Introduction: Unloved and Endangered

When you think about bats, bees, frogs, and sharks, is your first thought "ugh," and your second "I could do without those"? Do you think of wolves as vicious and turtles as slow, boring, and generally useless? Do you think of corals at all?

At some point, you have probably felt misunderstood. You might have thought your parents or teachers just did not get you. Likewise, you have probably felt that you were judged unfairly at times or got an undeserved bad rap. Have you ever considered that maybe these animals are just misunderstood or are getting a bad rap? Maybe it is worth exploring whether the rap is deserved. You could be surprised.

Coral, bumblebees, bats, frogs, marine turtles, wolves, and sharks all share a few important characteristics. They are all endangered species, and all play a vital part in our ecosystem.

What Is an Endangered Species?

Endangered species are those whose numbers are so few or are declining so quickly that they may not be able to have enough offspring to ensure the survival of the species and are therefore in danger of extinction.

An endangered species is a population at risk of becoming extinct—disappearing forever. If you look up "extinction" in the dictionary, you will find the words "abolition," "wiping out," and "annihilation."

We hear about endangered species all the time. Most people are aware of, and generally concerned about, endangered large mammals. There are even campaigns to save certain high-profile animal groups. Campaigns like "save the panda" are popular, because everyone can relate to a cute, cuddly panda. The thought of the extinction of this species can get people motivated to do something about the problem.

But many people do not realize that the disappearance of a key species at any level of the food chain can pose a significant ecological problem. The entire ecosystem is thrown off balance even when little-known or underappreciated animals vanish.

When Is a Species Considered Extinct?

According to the Organisation for Economic Co-operation and Development, a species is considered extinct when it has not been seen in the wild in the past fifty years.[1] But the International Union for Conservation of Nature and Natural Resources has a more technical definition:

> A taxon [a group of living organisms] is Extinct when there is no reasonable doubt that the last individual has died. A taxon is presumed Extinct when exhaustive surveys in known and/or expected habitat, at appropriate times . . . throughout its historic range have failed to record an individual. Surveys should be over a time frame appropriate to the taxon's life cycle and life form.[2]

Why Should You Care?

Some people think that the extinction of an unknown or unpopular species does not concern them. They may want to rethink that. There are a number of reasons that suggest the extinction of any species affects us all.

The loss of a species is arguably important in and of itself, as the permanent loss of any animal group detracts from our ability to enjoy nature and deprives future generations of the opportunity to do so. The aesthetic value of an extinct animal species cannot be replaced.

We also lose the recreational value from particular animal groups when we fail to protect a species. Observing animals in their natural habitats is the most obvious lost benefit. And while some would argue whether it should properly be considered "sport," there is a large market for recreational hunting and fishing. Neither of these activities is possible, however, if the population level of a species seriously declines.

From a moral perspective, in terms of distinguishing right from wrong, it can be argued that humans are stewards of the environment, responsible for protecting and caring for our natural habitat and its inhabitants. Have we failed in that role when an entire species disappears, particularly where humans have had a negative impact on the environment and contributed to the threat? Do animals have rights that humans need to respect?

An endangered species is a population at risk of becoming extinct—disappearing forever.

If moral or recreational issues are not enough to catch our attention, perhaps an appeal to self-interest may do the trick. Many endangered species serve important roles, such as eating massive quantities of pesky insects that would otherwise flourish unchecked or ensuring seed dispersal and pollination, which

Who Decides If a Species Is Endangered?

The International Union for the Conservation of Nature (IUCN) is a worldwide body founded in 1948. It groups organisms at risk according to the likelihood that they will become extinct, using the following categories:

* extinct: last remaining member of the species has died (or is presumed to have died)
* extinct in the wild: members of the species are alive in captivity but not in nature
* critically endangered: has an extremely high risk of becoming extinct in the immediate future
* endangered: has a high risk of extinction in the near future
* vulnerable: has a high risk of extinction in the medium-near future
* conservation dependent: not severely threatened, but depends on conservation programs to survive
* near threatened: may become threatened in the near future
* least concern: not immediately at risk

In the United States, the U.S. Fish and Wildlife Service and the National Marine Fisheries Service are in charge of carrying out the Endangered Species Act, a 1973 law that aims to reverse the trend toward human-caused extinction of wildlife. They keep a list of endangered and threatened plants and animals.

provides much of our food supply. Imagine a world where mosquito populations blossomed without natural predators. Imagine a world where our food supply was limited to primarily grains.

It is generally accepted that when any element of the food chain is removed from an ecosystem, destabilization will result. The ripple effects of the disappearance of a species are significant. The extinction of any species invariably affects secondary species, causing population increases or decreases that lead to the loss of other species and ultimately fundamentally changing the ecosystem structure irreversibly.

Strong arguments have been made that one of the most important, but often overlooked, concerns with extinction is the loss of irreplaceable genetic material. Every species carries its own unique genetic material—DNA. As a result, each species can produce unique chemicals and serve as a valuable source of knowledge and medical discovery. Many breakthrough drugs have come from animal genetic material.

Maybe through understanding, we can begin to appreciate the important role of conservation and our part in that process.

The Evolution of Conservation

Extinction is not new. For millions of years, species have evolved. As a result, a certain rate of extinction is natural.

Introduction: Unloved and Endangered

Some people argue that because this is a natural phenomenon, there is no cause for worry. They suggest that the warnings are unfounded and accuse conservationists of suffering from Chicken Little complex (named for the fairy-tale character who thought the sky was falling when an acorn fell on her head). The concern today, however, is that over the last century and a half, rates of extinction have risen dramatically. The risk of species extinction is significantly higher than at any time in the history of the earth. If the current rate of extinction continues, it is estimated that millions of species could disappear within the next decade.[3]

Another important difference to keep in mind is that while extinction can be the effect of the process of natural selection, it is generally accepted that the current dramatic rise in the rate of extinction is being caused by humans through habitat destruction, overexploitation of species, introduction of alien species, pollution, soil contamination, greenhouse gases, and transmission of diseases. By contrast, previous periods of mass extinction were triggered by geologic or climatic events, such as volcanic activity and meteor strikes.[4]

Some believe we are now in phase two of the sixth extinction period. Phase one began from one hundred thousand years ago up to ten thousand years ago with the arrival of a new species brought about by the movement of humans to different parts of the world.

The dodo and the passenger pigeon (inset) are two animals that became extinct recently due to unlimited hunting.

Humans disrupted the ecological balance by entering new ecosystems that had no prior human inhabitants.[5]

The introduction of agriculture started phase two about ten thousand years ago. Previously, hunters and gatherers had to ensure that their local habitats could sustain them. That naturally led to built-in conservation motivation, whether they were conscious of it or not. If the bounty from a particular area got low, the settlement moved on. This allowed those regions an opportunity for regrowth and repopulation of plant and animal life.

With the advent of agriculture, however, humans did not necessarily have to rely on their interaction with naturally occurring other species for survival. They were no longer as concerned with "carrying capacity" of the land or local habitat—that is, how much life the environment could support; they could now live beyond a local ecosystem. With this freedom, there began to be overloads of carrying capacities, over-population, and increased stress on the environment. The domestication of wild animals also began at this time, along with the start of widespread habitat destruction through development, pollution, and the introduction of foreign species.

Conservation Attitudes

In a world that seemed to host infinite resources, it is not surprising that conservation was originally ignored

President Theodore Roosevelt rides into Yellowstone, the first national park. Roosevelt was an early champion of conservation.

or at least received little attention. To the extent that conservation eventually became an issue, it is also not surprising that early efforts were geared to species considered economically important. Not all endangered species were protected. In fact, the extinction of species regarded as pests was welcomed.

Even for those species deemed deserving of protection, the focus was on the species itself. In other words, to the extent that conservation efforts were made, they centered on saving the animal. There was little thought of habitat protection or the many other issues that we now know impact on the conservation of a species.

Since European settlement of North America, five distinct periods of attitudes toward conservation of the environment have been classified:

❊ The Tree Reserves Period (1670–1860): The French and British made efforts to ensure a steady supply of necessary timber.

❊ The Land Reserves Period (1860–1885): The state reserved the land and sold it as the only source of revenue for government.

❊ The Resource Reserve Period (1880–present): Land was preserved to create a variety of parks, forests, reserves, bird sanctuaries, and wildlife preserves.

❊ The Recreation Reserves Period (1885–present): Recreation facilities reserves were introduced and historic sites were established.

❊ Nature and Wilderness Reserves Period (1960–present): The emphasis has shifted to retaining areas to allow nature to shape the environment, rather than for resource use or recreation. There is recognition of the value of preserving parts of the environment in its natural state.[6]

Conservation in North America

President Theodore Roosevelt kick-started the American conservation movement in the early 1900s. Interestingly, Canadians maintained the myth of limitless resources longer than their American counterparts. As the United States settled and developed more quickly, Americans were initially ahead of Canadians with respect to conservation.[7]

Is Conservation Important?

Although there is disagreement about how we should react to the problem, it is generally accepted that the environment is currently at risk. One study indicated that if humans continue to destroy habitats at the current pace, it will take 10 million years to recover.[8] Perhaps humans will not survive at all. It has been suggested that "even if we behave well from now on, we will lose ten percent of the world's species this century and if we behave badly, we'll lose fifty percent."[9]

Similarly, the reasons put forward for conservation are very different. Some people believe that nature has intrinsic value—that is, that each plant and animal has its own value above and beyond its usefulness to humans. Some believe that conserving biodiversity is all about ensuring genetic variety, species, habitats, and ecosystems, while others see conservation as a political, economic, or social issue. Either way, we are learning that the loss of any species can have a profound impact on the workings of an ecosystem as a whole. The ripple effects are far-reaching and often unanticipated.

Clearly there is tension between conservation and development. But, regardless of the motivations for conservation, the fact is we need clean water, we need clean air, we need food, we need stable soils to protect against natural catastrophes—in short, we need biodiversity to ensure the continuance of the human race. We need to find a way to balance the competing interests and protect our environment, if only to protect ourselves.

Aboriginal Perspective

An Australian Gagudju account of creation teaches:
The Earth is our mother, the eagle our cousin. The tree draws blood from us and the grass is growing. Our ancestors told us: Now that we have done all these things, you must watch over them and ensure that they are forever. It is in this way that human beings became the custodians of the planet.[10]

2

In Search of Nemo: Coral Reefs

What is coral? Does a deep pink color come to mind? Or is it jewelry—perhaps a necklace, bracelet, or earrings? Actually, corals are marine animals that produce a calcium carbonate skeleton beneath their film of living tissue.

Have you ever been snorkeling or seen underwater shots of a coral reef? It is a beautiful, breathtaking experience. The coral reefs provide a feast for the eyes, with their incredible variety of color, shape, and texture. Some seem formidable and imposing, some delicate and wispy. From waving fans or intricate branches to wrinkly brains, they host a myriad of creatures and spill over with life. Almost one thousand coral species currently exist. It is widely believed today, however, that our corals are in crisis,

Coral in an artificial reef in one of the Chuuk islands in the South Pacific

and their decline could have profound impact on our ecosystem. Recognizing that we need to consider the problem and examine future prospects, 2008 was declared the International Year of the Reef.

What Is a Coral Reef?

Corals have been described as "thin amounts of tissue on top of a rock that they build."[1] Many people think of the entire reef as coral, but in reality, the reef structure itself is generally coral skeletal remains. Only a thin layer of coral polyps on the reef's surface is actually alive. These tiny polyps build protective shells around themselves to ward off predators. As new polyps are born, they build their shells on top of the skeletons of their predecessors, and as these layers of limestone shells grow over the years, they form a coral reef. Fragmented skeletons fill in the spaces between the larger dead coral branches.

Types of Coral Reefs

Coral reefs are generally divided into four main types:

1. Atolls
* where reefs form a ring around a lagoon
* mainly found in the Indian and Pacific oceans

2. Barrier
* separated from the mainland by a deep channel or lagoon

3. Platform
* usually lie in sheltered seas and quite far offshore
* flat-topped with small, shallow lagoons

4. Fringing
* most common
* directly attached to land or separated by a shallow lagoon, forming a border along the shoreline and surrounding islands

The skeletons become the material forming the reef structure, as new corals grow in conjunction with symbiotic, or cooperative, algae. The algae get shelter and food from the polyp, and the polyp gets food in return through photosynthesis. As each is dependent on the other, the colony actually functions as a plant-animal combination.

Coral reefs are the largest and oldest living systems on the earth. While growth rates of various coral species and reef structures differ, overall coral reefs are exceptionally slow to develop. Massive corals grow at only about ten millimeters (.4 inches) per year. Some branching and staghorn corals can add approximately ten centimeters (four inches) per year. Either way, they form huge structures over incredibly long periods of time. The Great Barrier Reef, for example, was formed over a span of 5 million years.[2]

Coral reefs are the largest and oldest living systems on the earth.

Why Does Coral Matter?

Coral reefs are often referred to as the rain forests of the sea. It is not only the diversity of corals themselves but also the millions of species they house that make coral reefs such critical ecosystems. It is no wonder that coral reefs are considered among the most biologically important marine environments and one of the most productive, complex, and species-rich marine ecosystems.

Coral reefs house over 25 percent of all known marine fish, with some reefs serving as home to up to one thousand different species in a single square meter.[3] Some estimates suggest that there are up to 2 million species found in, on, and around all coral reefs.[4]

Role of Coral Reefs

Coral reefs serve a number of important functions.

Food and income. Microscopic algae and bacteria coat coral and exposed surfaces of a reef. These are grazed by large populations of fish. In turn, millions of people in developing countries depend on these reefs as a source of food and income. According to the "Status of Coral Reefs of the World 2002" report by the Global Coral Reef Monitoring Network, cosponsored by the United Nations Environment Programme, "Coral reef ecosystems provide a global total of thirty five billion dollars ($35 billion) a year in goods and services, with about 500 million people dependent on them for food, materials, or income."[5]

In the South Pacific, reef and lagoon fish account for 29 percent of commercial local fishing in addition to supplying the local food source. In fact, according to the Australian Institute of Marine Science, it is believed that "up to 90% of the animal protein consumed on many Pacific islands comes from marine sources."[6]

The living matter produced in a coral reef system is believed to be between 30 to 250 times greater than that of the open ocean.[7]

Homes. In addition to providing food, coral reefs literally serve as home to millions of people. Two and a half million people live on Pacific islands built by coral or surrounded by coral reefs. An additional three hundred thousand people live on coral islands in the Indian Ocean.[8]

Protector of land. Coral reefs also provide important protective barriers. Acting like seawalls, they form natural breakwaters that shelter lagoons and protect coastlines against wave damage, storm surges, and erosion.

Filters. We do not usually drink our water directly from oceans, lakes, rivers, or streams. We filter it through sophisticated filtering systems and devices. Similarly, our water bodies need filtering systems. According to Stephen Palumbi, a marine biologist at Stanford University, "Healthy reef communities are great filters with invertebrates that basically spend their lives filtering the water."[9] Large marine reef sponges, for example, serve as

Coral reefs are crucial to the survival of undersea creatures, since they house more than a quarter of all known marine fish.

microbial filters. So with the loss of coral reefs, we lose nature's purification system.

Tourism and recreation. Coral reefs now support a massive tourism and recreation industry, as people come from around the world to hot vacation spots to check out nature's underwater parks. A multibillion-dollar industry offers snorkeling, scuba diving, and fishing off the bounties of the coral reef system. In addition to income from these direct activities surrounding the reefs, the hotel, restaurant, and travel industries depend on the continued viability of coral reefs. This is another example of the ripple effects of this important ecosystem.

Source of Knowledge

Because corals are very sensitive to temperature, they are now believed to be ideal indicators of climate change. Scientists can explore past climate and environmental conditions on particular reefs by examining annual bands on some corals, much like reading tree rings.

Coral reefs and dependent ocean ecosystems are also a huge source of potential medicines. Incredibly, there are over a million microorganisms in a single drop of seawater alone. Just imagine the untold and undiscovered source of plant and animal species that may hold the secret to disease treatments. There are already many examples of important drugs being used today based on material from marine ecosystems. Materials from marine sponges, for example, are used in drugs for HIV/AIDS treatment. Many believe that marine biotechnology is on the verge of a breakthrough with new anticancer agents that activate the immune system and inhibit cancer cell growth.[10]

In addition to pharmaceutical use, coral reefs are a source of orthopedic, cosmetic, and surgical implants created from coral skeletons.

Human and Other Threats

It would be easy to assume that because corals are high producers—in terms of the living matter produced by the plants and algae in a coral reef system—they are not at imminent risk. Similarly, it would be easy to assume that because coral reefs often look like massive rock structures, they are hardy and durable. But it would be a mistake to make these assumptions. In fact, the Australian Institute of Marine Science warns that though reefs are highly productive, the "amount of organic matter that can be taken out of the reef whether by harvesting or other means without causing damage to the community remains severely limited."[11] The fact is, coral reef systems are very fragile.

It is estimated that 30 percent of coral reefs around the world are "severely damaged" and that up to 60 percent could be lost by 2030.[12] Studies suggest that there has been a dramatic increase in the amount of reef damage in the past few decades. It stands to reason that if this rate of destruction continues, the coral reefs will be in crisis.

As coral reefs grow close to the sea surface, they are highly sensitive to environmental changes in the air, land, and sea. Population growth and technology are two key factors contributing to coral reef decline. The reefs are threatened by domestic, agricultural, and industrial waste pouring into ocean waters. Ironically, the very tourism industry that depends on income generated from coral reefs can degrade the reef when sewage and other waste are allowed to pollute reef areas or when resorts are situated so as to increase beach erosion.

Similarly, poor land-use practices can increase sedimentation—the settling of matter at the bottom of a body of water—and detract from the health of the reef. Deforestation, for example, leads to soil erosion, and loads of sediment wash over the coral reefs.

Add to that the damage caused by swimmers, snorkelers, divers, boat anchors, and sport fishers. Similarly, the collection of aquarium fish and live corals is a lucrative market that is damaging the reefs on which they depend. Believe it or not, cyanide is sometimes used to force fish out from the coral and allow easy capture. It is no wonder that more than half the fish harvested in this way die before reaching the market.[13]

Overexploitation of reef resources puts unmanageable strain on the reefs, but unfortunately it is often not noticed until the problem has reached critical stages. As the fish population dwindles through overfishing, people resort to destructive practices, such as harvesting with dynamite and poison. These obviously pose a serious

An elkhorn coral colony in the Florida Keys. It is estimated that 60 percent of the world's coral reefs could be gone by 2030.

threat to the viability of the coral reef ecosystems.[14] Overfishing itself is problematic, because the removal of fish and other grazers allows algae to compete with, and smother, young corals and accelerates the degradation of the reef.

Global Climate Change

There is much talk today about global warming and climate change. What impact does this have on coral reefs? Many scientists predict that over the next century, we will see higher world temperatures and a climate change rate greater than anything we have seen in over six thousand years.[15] We know that even small increases in temperature above normal local maximums can cause coral bleaching. In response to stress, coral polyps expel the cooperative algae, and as a result, the corals die.

While local stresses are clearly the greatest imminent threat to the viability of coral reef systems, the long-term threat of climate change may be more significant for human populations. The World Conservation Union states: "While corals and reef communities can recover from severe episodic disasters such as cyclones and storms, they are vulnerable to many low-level but continuing chronic stresses created by human populations."[16] As humans degrade local reefs through the practices identified above, a Global Task Team of experts observed that "remote reefs will become critical to serve as refuges for coral reef biodiversity."[17] With climate change impacting these remote reefs, that safeguard is jeopardized.

Impact

Coral reefs have suffered a worldwide dramatic decline in recent years, with about 10 percent already possibly degraded beyond recovery and another 30 percent likely to suffer serious decline within the next two decades. Unless we recognize the urgency of implementing effective management of these important resources, it is estimated that over two-thirds of the world's coral reefs may collapse ecologically within the next generation.[18]

Future

There is no magic wand to wave and no single way to ensure coral conservation. The problem is complex, and we will have to monitor the health of coral reefs and their communities more systematically than before. It would be smart to listen to indigenous people who have been taking care of their natural resources for centuries. Many Pacific Island cultures, for example, developed traditional conservation and management systems to control overexploitation long before North American and European biologists, and they promoted the idea by limiting and controlling access.[19] They enforced rules that conserved fishery stocks on small coral reefs.

Although there are many causes of coral die-off, it is clear that coral reefs represent an important resource, both in terms of global biological diversity and with respect to the well-being of the people who depend on them. While they have survived over geologic time, it is also clear that they are now vulnerable to the combined stresses of human overexploitation and climate change. But though threatened, reefs are salvageable.[20] The challenge to scientists, managers, national bodies, international programs, and all of us is to work together to preserve the reefs of the world.

3

Bees—What's the Buzz?

f a bee crashes a party or picnic, there is likely to be some swatting, some running, and probably a few screams. Even the buzz of a bee can cause a panic.

And when people think of pollen, it normally brings to mind allergies, complete with runny eyes, red noses, and sneezes. Few people are thankful that bees pollinate plants that provide much of our food. If you associate bees with stings or honey, you are not alone. In a survey of visitors to the National Zoological Park's pollination exhibit, most people associated bees with stings or honey production, not pollination.[1]

What Is Pollination?

Have you ever heard of the "birds and the bees" speech and wondered why it is called that? Well, some birds and most bees are pollinators, and pollination is the way flowering plants reproduce. You may remember from science class that plants need a helper to get pollen from the anther, the male part of one flower, to the stigma, the receptive female surface of another flower. Bees, and other pollinators, are those helpers.

Some plants get help by throwing their pollen to the wind, so to speak. But most wind-pollinated plants tend to be boring, like grains and cereals. Because there was no need to attract a pollinator, they were small, dull, and odorless. But it is believed that millions of years ago,

A bumblebee pollinating a flower. An estimated 90 percent of the world's flowering plants require pollinators such as bees.

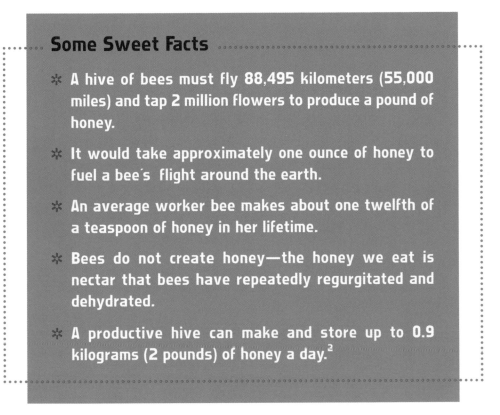

Some Sweet Facts

* A hive of bees must fly 88,495 kilometers (55,000 miles) and tap 2 million flowers to produce a pound of honey.

* It would take approximately one ounce of honey to fuel a bee's flight around the earth.

* An average worker bee makes about one twelfth of a teaspoon of honey in her lifetime.

* Bees do not create honey—the honey we eat is nectar that bees have repeatedly regurgitated and dehydrated.

* A productive hive can make and store up to 0.9 kilograms (2 pounds) of honey a day.[2]

plants began adapting to recruit pollinators. Flowers had to get a makeover and give off noticeable smells to attract new pollinators.[3]

But what was the payoff for the pollinators? Being pretty is just not enough. Plants needed to offer up something extra. And so it is that plants produce sweet nectar. Pollinators come looking for nectar, get dusted with pollen, and carry it to deposit on another plant along the way, and so starts the fertilization and reproduction process. Everyone is a winner.

Through evolution, plants and animals responded to each other's needs, adapting to coexist in a mutually beneficial arrangement. Bees have jokingly been referred to as "flying Swiss Army knives" by entomologists, because of the number of adaptations they have developed to access new or changing flower structures.[4] But there is concern that some of these relationships are so specialized that the loss of one species is likely to threaten the existence of the other species.

The Role of Bees

Bees are key pollinators. One in every three bites of food that hits your mouth comes thanks to bees' pollination efforts. About 90 percent of the world's two hundred fifty thousand flowering plant species, including at least eight hundred species that are cultivated by humans for food, need pollinators.[5] Our food supply is dependent on the productivity of bees as pollinators.

Honeybees are the best-known pollinators, and they are the most widely studied and recorded, but they are more selfish than their cousin the bumblebee. Honeybees will not pollinate flowers that do not produce nectar, but bumblebees will. Honeybees are also unable to pollinate some of our most important agricultural crops, including tomatoes, blueberries, cranberries, eggplant, chili peppers, and kiwis, to name just a few.

Bumblebees and a few species of solitary bees have the ability to "buzz pollinate"—they grab flower petals with their mandibles and vibrate their flight muscles two hundred to five hundred times per second, holding tightly with their legs without moving their wings. To give you some idea how fast that is, try flexing your biceps and see how many flexes you can do in one second. Now imagine doing that hundreds of times faster. The vibration is so strong that bumblebees have been likened to living tuning forks as they give off a loud buzz

Honeybees will not pollinate flowers that do not produce nectar, but bumblebees will.

"in the range of middle C."[6] Buzz pollination is essential for about 9 percent of flowering plants, making bees an important link in our food supply.

In addition to pollinating strawberries, eggplants, peppers, cabbage, and carrots, bumblebees are the chief pollinators of red clover and alfalfa. These are used to feed animals that supply meat and dairy products, so we depend on pollinators directly and indirectly for our food.

Bees in Danger

Bee populations currently face a number of threats, causing a serious drop in their numbers. In fact, all

Who Needs Bees?

What do onions, blueberries, and carrots have in common? All three crops rely almost exclusively on bees for pollination. The following are some of the top ten crops dependent on honeybees. (All figures refer to total production in 2006.)

* 81 percent of the sweet cherry crop in the United States—$380 million worth—is pollinated by bees.

* 27 percent of the oranges grown in the United States are pollinated by bees and are worth around $478 million.

* The blueberry crop is almost entirely reliant on honeybees for pollination—90 percent of blueberries in the United States are pollinated by bees. These crops are worth $502 million.

* Like blueberries, carrots are reliant on bees for pollination—90 percent of the carrot crop in the United States is pollinated by bees and is worth $519 million.

* 90 percent of the broccoli crop in the United States—worth an estimated $588 million—is reliant on bees for pollination.

* 90 percent of the onion crop in the United States is reliant on bees for pollination. These crops are worth $781 million.

* An astonishing 100 percent of the almond crop is pollinated by bees and is worth about $2 billion.[7]

pollinators are vulnerable, with habitat loss and pesticides topping the threat list. Because of the number of crops dependent on pollination, as bees and other pollinators disappear at an alarming rate, our fruits and vegetables will likely be in jeopardy. Some people have gone so far as to call the problem a "pollination crisis."[8]

Beekeepers throughout the United States report significant losses of their honeybee hives. In 2007, bees suddenly disappeared by the billions in a phenomenon dubbed colony collapse disorder (CCD). The mysterious vanishing act had experts, conservationists, and bee-keepers alike confused and concerned. Though the problem was not fully understood, and there was no definitive answer as to the cause of the crisis, it is generally agreed that pesticide contamination, an unknown disease, and mites are likely factors contributing to CCD.

Another identified "suspect" is travel—the stress on bees from increased migratory pollination (where bee-keepers travel from coast to coast, hiring out their bees as pollinators). As their natural habitat is eliminated through development, bees disappear, leaving no one to pollinate the crops. Ironically, farmers sometimes cut down the forested area that houses the bees to make way for more planting fields, only to find the crops cannot flourish because the pollinators are gone. They then have to rent bees at significant cost.

A beekeeper works at his hives. In 2007, American beekeepers reported that honeybees were disappearing by the millions.

Bees—What's the Buzz?

Traveling leaves the bees vulnerable to new diseases and insecticides. Importation of foreign bees carries risks of pest and parasite introduction, and competition from introduced bees threatens native pollinators. Many bee colonies and populations have been wiped out or seriously diminished because of the introduction of viral diseases and parasites such as mites.[9]

Bees are sensitive to chemicals, and pesticides can be fatal. In fact, we have seen a decline of more than 50 percent in the number of honeybees. Pests, pesticides, disease, and habitat loss have been blamed.[10] Whatever the culprit, if a solution cannot be found, it is estimated that 80 percent of fruits and vegetables requiring pollination will be lost.[11]

Worker bees are famous for always acting in the best interest of the hive. For that reason, sick bees generally leave the hive to die to avoid the risk of infecting their hive-mates. Research suggests that bees are suffering from immune-suppressing diseases.[12] Is that the cause of the disappearance of large numbers of bees? Are the bees sacrificing themselves for the good of the hive?

Some people argue that the large-scale disappearance of the bees is just part of a natural cycle and that concern is unjustified, or at least exaggerated. But while there is some evidence of historical disappearances of large bee populations that recovered naturally, most agree that the current problem is unprecedented both in terms of scope and suddenness.

Humans directly impact the loss of pollinating bees by destroying habitats. "We're losing six thousand acres of habitat a day to development, 365 days a year," notes Orley Taylor, a professor of insect ecology at the University of Kansas.[13] Taylor successfully lobbied for a National Pollinator Week and convinced the U.S. Postal Service to put out a block of four "Pollination" stamps, including a bumblebee, hummingbird, bat, and butterfly.

The Future

Researchers are working on management of diseases and containment of imported species. The two issues go hand in hand, since the importation of foreign bees introduces the risk of new diseases and insecticides.

Reducing or eliminating the use of pesticides is an important first step in protecting our bee populations. Gardeners, farmers, and homeowners alike can use alternative nontoxic methods to control pests and weeds.

Gardeners can also play a role by creating habitats for pollinators. Even if you do not have a green thumb, learning to be tolerant of wildflowers and plant species sometimes thought of as weeds can be an important step toward pollinators' survival. We need to remember that if we get rid of the plants that attract bees and other pollinators, we endanger the bee populations as well.

Bees must tap 2 million flowers to produce a pound of honey; a productive hive can make up to two pounds of honey per day.

Yet, while numerous plants are on the endangered species list, interestingly, only one in fifteen plants has even had its pollinators identified, let alone protected.[14]

Consider purchasing organic produce. As more people switch to organic produce, it will provide economic incentives for growers to switch to organic farming methods, which are more pollinator friendly.

What Can You Do?

You can make a difference for bees:

* ❋ Create a pollinator-friendly habitat in your yard.
* ❋ Plant for pollinators in your yard, garden, farm, and local community.
* ❋ Reduce your impact on the environment.
* ❋ Learn about pollinators, and spread the word.
* ❋ Ask your parents to buy organic products.[15]

Bees are amazing creatures. Aerodynamically, bumblebees should not be able to fly. They baffle and intrigue scientists and engineers as they defy gravity. But if you do not believe that bees are beautiful and intriguing and deserve protection in their own right, then perhaps you will be convinced of the importance of their conservation for ecological or economic reasons. Either way, next time you hear a bee buzz by, don't be afraid—just say, "Thanks for all the hard work!"

4

I Think I'm Going Batty: Bats

When you think of bats, do you picture dark castles and Dracula? Does the thought of bats swooping in your yard give you goose bumps? Unlike Dracula, bats play a vital role in the circle of life. They are much misunderstood and maligned creatures of the night. In fact, it has been said that bats may be the most misunderstood animals in the United States.

Amazing Diversity

With more than eleven hundred different bat species worldwide, bats account for almost a quarter of all mammal species. In fact, bats are found on every continent except Antarctica. Most people have a stereotypical image of a bat, but the reality is that bats' diversity is amazing, ranging from the world's smallest mammal, the bumblebee bat of

Amazing Bat Facts
Did you know?

* Bat droppings in caves support whole ecosystems of unique organisms, including bacteria used in detoxifying wastes, improving detergents, and producing fuels and antibiotics.

* An anticoagulant from vampire bat saliva may soon be used to treat humans with heart disease.

* African heart-nosed bats can hear the footsteps of a beetle walking on sand from a distance of more than 1.8 meters (six feet).[1]

Thailand, weighing in at less than a penny, to some flying fox bats with 1.8-meter (six-foot) wingspans. Some are furry, some not; some dull, some brightly colored; some even have pink ears and wings, while others are patterned. Whatever their appearance, one thing is for certain: Bats play an important role in our ecosystem.

Bat Myths

There are a number of myths about bats. Which of the following have you heard?

I Think I'm Going Batty: Bats

Bats are a health risk to humans because they carry rabies. While it is true that bats can contract rabies, as can any mammal, the reality is that very few do. In fact, less than half of one percent of bats contract rabies, and, perhaps more importantly, unlike many other animals, even rabid bats rarely become aggressive. To put it in context, bat rabies is responsible for approximately one human death per year in the United States. By contrast, dog attacks or contact are responsible for almost ten times that amount. Worldwide, dogs are the more common carriers of rabies. An estimated fifty thousand humans die annually of rabies; the majority of these deaths follow bites from infected dogs.[2] In fact, pets, sports, and even playground equipment are considerably more dangerous than bats.[3]

Bats are blind. Contrary to popular belief, bats are not blind. In fact, many have excellent vision. However, bats can also "see" using sound alone. They can communicate and navigate using echolocation: a sonar navigation system in which bats emit pulses of high-frequency sound (inaudible to humans) and can identify and locate objects in their path by listening to the echoes reflected back to them. Even in total darkness they can detect and avoid obstacles as fine as a human hair. This ability is still not fully understood even by current scientists, and

Some say bats are the most misunderstood animals in the United States.

has been estimated to be billions of times more efficient than any similar system developed by humans.[4]

Bats get tangled in people's hair. Because of bats' ability to echolocate so accurately, they may fly very close to someone's face while insect hunting, but they do not get stuck in people's hair.

Bats are rodents. Bats may look somewhat like rodents, but they are not. In fact, recent evidence suggests that bats may be more closely related to primates (including humans) than rodents.[5]

Bats suck people's blood. The Dracula legend has given the infamous vampire bats a bad rap. In reality, vampire bats are quite small, weighing only an ounce. They do feed on the blood of warm-blooded animals, but they do not suck blood. Rather, the bats make a small cut in the skin of a sleeping animal and lap up the blood that flows from the wound. Incredibly, there is an anticoagulant in bats' saliva that prevents the animal's blood from clotting until the bat finishes its meal.[6] This anticoagulant may soon be used to treat human heart patients.

Bats in Danger

Dramatic reductions in bat populations are occurring worldwide. This is of particular concern because bats are very vulnerable to extinction. For their size, they are the

A flying fox, or fruit bat. More than 50 percent of
American bat species are in severe decline.

slowest reproducing mammals on the earth; in most species, bats produce only one offspring per year. Over 50 percent of American bat species are already listed as endangered or in severe decline.[7]

Bats have every reason to fear humans. Humans are harming bats through the use of pesticides and other chemical toxins, habitat destruction, direct killing, vandalism, and disturbance of hibernating and maternity colonies. Few animals consume bats as a regular part of their diet, leaving humans as the only animal significantly negatively impacting bats.

When hibernating bats are awakened, they use up valuable winter fat needed to support them until spring. It is estimated that a single arousal can cost a bat as much energy as it would normally use in two to three weeks of hibernation. So, if hibernating bats are disturbed often, they may starve to death before spring. As a result, human disturbance of hibernation colonies is a serious problem and threat. However well intentioned, even cavers and biologists can cause these disturbances and put the colonies at risk.

Similarly, human disturbance to maternity colonies is dangerous. Mother bats do not tolerate interference

> **Over 50 percent of American bat species are already listed as endangered or in severe decline.**

when flightless newborn are present. If disturbances occur, panicked mothers may abandon or drop baby bats to their death.[8]

There have been serious large-scale bat disappearances in which entire colonies of bats are devastated, leaving experts shaking their heads as to the cause. It was noted that the bat die-off had "eerie similarities with 'colony collapse disorder,'"[9] which decimated bee populations. Recently, a mysterious new disease known as white nose syndrome has killed thousands of bats in the northeastern United States. "Most bat researchers would agree that this is the gravest threat to bats they have ever seen," said Alan Hicks of the New York Department of Environmental Conservation.[10] Studies confirm that some bat species are in trouble already, and the trend continues.[11]

Why Should You Care?

Bats are considered "keystone" species in the lives of plants crucial to entire ecosystems. The seed dispersal and pollination activities of fruit- and nectar-eating bats are critical to the survival of rain forests. Tropical bats are invaluable in their reforestation role. It is estimated that up to 95 percent of forest regrowth is attributable to seeds dropped by bats.[12]

Further, a decline in bat populations could have a profound effect on our food supplies. Like bees, bats

I Think I'm Going Batty: Bats

A bat colony in an underground cave. Even in total darkness, bats can use echolocation to avoid obstacles.

are key pollinators responsible for helping to pollinate the 250,000 species of flowering plants that need pollinating. Popular commercial products such as bananas, avocados, dates, figs, peaches, mangoes, and cashews rely on bats for survival. Many plant species depend almost completely on bats for pollination. These plants bloom at night and use odors and special shapes to attract bats. An example is the famous baobab tree of the African savannas. The baobab is sometimes considered the "tree of life," given how critical it is to the survival of other wildlife. Only bats are likely to

Welcome to My Home!

Bat survival is threatened by the lack of suitable roosting sites. Consider buying or building a bat house to entice these little insect-eating mammals to share your yard. Is it safe? Statistically, hosting a bat house is safer than owning a dog. Here are some helpful tips to increase the odds of getting bats to make your bat house their home.

* Do not mount your bat house close to bright lights.

* Use untreated wood; pressure-treated wood can contain harmful chemicals.

* Houses mounted on trees are more difficult for bats to find; they are also more vulnerable to predators. Try a pole or the side of a building.

* Avoid areas with obstacles, such as tree branches. Give the bats a clear swoop zone.

* Make sure the inside of the house is roughened to give bats grip—create horizontal grooves.

* Temperature is an important factor in bat roost selection; try to ensure that the bat house receives direct sun each day.

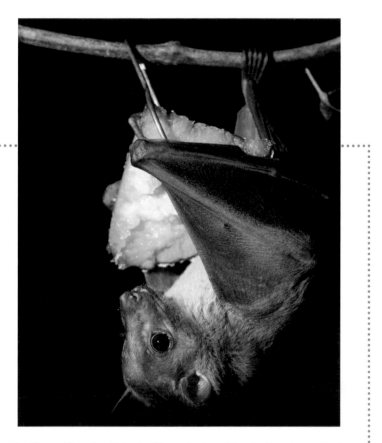

An Egyptian fruit bat. The study of bats has resulted in a great deal of information helpful to humans.

achieve pollination, since they approach from below, seeking nectar, and are able to contact the flower's reproductive organs.

Bats also play an important role in the balance of nature, because they are the primary predators of night-flying insects. They consume massive quantities of insects that are at best annoying yard pests or, perhaps more importantly, costly agricultural pests. A single bat can eat up to one thousand insects in one hour. Large colonies of bats eat literally tons of insects nightly. That is many times more effective than even the best bug zapper on the market.

Although getting rid of those annoying mosquitoes may be reason enough to want to conserve bats, the loss of bats also causes a ripple effect; without bats to control insect populations, the demand for chemical pesticides increases dramatically. This jeopardizes other plant and animal ecosystems and ultimately human health and human livelihood.

The study of bats has resulted in a rich store of knowledge in a number of areas, including the development of navigational aids for the blind, birth control and artificial insemination techniques, vaccine production, surgical procedures, and drug testing.[13]

Recognizing the need to protect these valuable creatures, Bat Conservation International, in conjunction with industry groups, has initiated a program in which more than a thousand former U.S. mines have been turned into bat sanctuaries. These new "caves" have seen dramatic increases in colony populations.[14]

So the next time you think of bats swooping through your yard, say, "Thanks, it's great to see you!" Maybe you could even build them a bat house.

5

Someday My Prince Will Come: Frogs

In folklore, frogs are generally portrayed as ugly and slimy. When they are not hopping off lily pads or singing "ribbit" in the pond, frogs are said to turn into beautiful princes or princesses if you kiss them. Well, what would you think of a world where there were no frogs to kiss? If your answer was "big deal," perhaps you should think again. The fact is that frogs are disappearing at an alarming rate, and their disappearance is cause for concern. Evidence shows that amphibians have been in decline globally for the last half century.

What Is an Amphibian?

Amphibians, like reptiles, are a class of cold-blooded vertebrate, including frogs, toads, salamanders, and newts.

A red-eyed tree frog climbing on bamboo

Most lay eggs and undergo metamorphosis, as they move from a larval stage, which is usually aquatic, through the development of limbs and lungs, to become terrestrial as adults.

Almost all amphibian species are dependent on moist conditions, and many require freshwater habitats to breed. One of the features that distinguish amphibians from other creatures is their permeable skin. Tiny holes allow moisture from the air or ground to pass through the porous skin, keeping the creature moist. They also "breathe" oxygen through their skin. The problem with

Fascinating Frog Facts

Did you know?

* Amphibians must shed their skin as they enlarge in size. The old skin is taken off like a piece of clothing that has become too tight. Usually they eat the shed skin.

* Frogs absorb water through their skin, so they do not need to drink.

* Like a tree, frog bones form a growth ring every year when the frog is hibernating. Scientists can count these rings to discover the age of the frog.[1]

this feature, though, is that while useful, it also leaves them vulnerable. This sensitive skin renders them much more likely to be impacted by pollution and other environmental hazards.

Amphibians live their lives on both land and water, hence the name *amphibian*, meaning "double life."

Dangers Frogs Face

Of the 6,420 known species of amphibians in the world, including frogs, toads, and salamanders, about half those species are declining in number, and nearly one third are threatened with extinction.[2] There is no one single threat causing the significant worldwide decrease in frog populations; a variety of threats are affecting amphibian species.

Habitat loss or modification. Habitat loss has an obvious direct impact in reducing frog populations. Whether through forestry operations or clear-cutting for development, frogs are losing their homes at a rapid rate. Whole cities and suburbs now exist where frogs used to sing out their nightly chorus.

Modification of frog habitats also causes direct population declines. Draining wetlands, for example, removes breeding grounds and fragments, or splits, frog populations, increasing the chance of regional extinction. Water is critical to frog survival. Frogs breed in water, their young develop and are raised in it, and some frogs even hibernate in it. As a result, the massive draining of wetlands for farmland or urban growth is devastating. In southern Ontario, for example, 90 percent of wetlands have been drained.[3] Consider for a moment if all but 10 percent of the housing in your neighborhood disappeared almost overnight. Where would all the people go? Would you be surprised to see a serious population decline in the area?

Even in areas where good habitats remain, habitat fragmentation can still cause population declines. In other words, when connections between ponds are interfered with, the normal immigration between frog populations cannot continue. As a result, these small groups die out.[4]

In a worldwide Global Amphibian Assessment, it was found that habitat loss and degradation were the greatest threat to amphibians, affecting almost four thousand species. In fact, this threat was four times greater than the next most common threat: pollution.[5]

Toxins. Environmental toxins can not only kill frogs directly, they can also have serious indirect impacts on reproduction, disrupting normal development, reducing growth rates, and increasing susceptibility to disease.

Exposure to pesticides and synthetic fertilizers can prevent tadpoles from developing, poison juvenile frogs, and alter adult frogs' hormones.[6] There are increasing

A Pine Barrens tree frog. A variety of environmental changes threaten frog populations, including habitat loss.

reports of frog deformities, believed to be caused by environmental toxins. There have been some reports of 70 percent of frog populations with malformations.[7]

Frogs are more susceptible than many other species to environmental toxins as a result of their permeable skin and so are more vulnerable to pollution.

Disease. A number of diseases have been reported as causing mass mortality of frog populations. Various fungi have also been linked to mass deaths of frogs through infections. The disappearance of the harlequin frogs from Monteverde Cloud Forest Preserve in Costa Rica raised serious concerns. Scientists were baffled about the die-off of these frogs in such a protected environment. After decades of study, it is now believed that global warming may be making frogs more susceptible to disease. As one scientist put it, "Disease is the bullet killing frogs, but climate change is pulling the trigger."[8]

Climate. Changes in local weather conditions as a result of global climate change can impact on frogs' ecology in a number of ways. Generally, it is argued that a warming world is likely to cause higher mortality among amphibians.[9] Studies suggest that dry conditions associated with climate change are responsible for "alarming shifts in population patterns."[10] Evidence suggests that earlier spawning (egg production) occurs and that climate change encourages outbreaks of certain pathogens.

Reductions in water depths as a result of declining precipitation and altered weather patterns expose frog embryos to damaging ultraviolet-B radiation, believed to cause lethal fungus infections. According to an expert at the Golden Toad Laboratory for Conservation, embryos appear to "develop normally for a few days, but then turn white and die by the hundreds of thousands."[11]

Ultraviolet radiation. You are no doubt familiar with the UV index. All summer long we hear forecasts about the UV rating for the day. We are careful to use sunscreen lotion if it is particularly high. There has been much talk about the dangers of decreased ozone allowing more UV radiation to reach the earth. Skin cancers are certainly on the rise. Frogs cannot protect themselves from this increased UV exposure. In particular, eggs seem vulnerable, with decreased hatching of frog eggs resulting from increased UV exposure.

Predation. Larval frogs are particularly vulnerable to predators. While predation is normal and part of the necessary ecological life cycle, the introduction of predatory fish seriously increases the exposure of native amphibians to predators they are not accustomed to. Larval frogs that coexist with neighboring predators have evolved "antipredator mechanisms," or ways to help protect themselves against predator attacks. These changes include tadpole coloring and patterning or swimming behavior and are geared to protect against a particular known predator. When new, unfamiliar predators, such as gamefish, mosquitofish, or crayfish, are introduced, native amphibians that are exposed to them have not developed appropriate responses or defenses. The introduction of farmed bullfrogs has been blamed for serious frog population declines in the western United States. Bullfrogs are voracious predators of their smaller cousins. Without the skills to protect against these new predators, frogs are dying in higher numbers. Many amphibians can only survive in fish-free waters. In fact, the introduction of predatory fish into what is

Someday My Prince Will Come: Frogs

These frog eggs are vulnerable to ultraviolet radiation, which has increased recently because of damage to the ozone layer that protects the earth.

normally fish-free water can cause rapid extinction of frogs and other amphibians.[12]

Humans are also predators. In some countries, frog populations have been decimated for the frog-leg trade. Frogs are also used for medicines, bait, and biology classes.

Traffic mortality. With development comes traffic. As frogs try to cross roads to get to breeding ponds or travel between habitats, they are routinely run over. Along a single two-mile stretch of highway in southern

Ontario, for example, over ten thousand leopard frogs were killed in a single year.[13]

Why Should You Care?

At first blush, frogs may seem outright ugly. But in fact, many species are resplendent in their vibrant colors. If the sight of frogs does nothing for you, consider the awesome sound and variety of their croaking chorus at night. It is hard to believe so much noise can come from such little animals. Leaving aside the sight and sounds, frogs can be just plain interesting. Many kids get their first exposure to wildlife through their interactions with frogs—trying to catch them or watching their tadpoles develop almost like magic.

If none of this gives you warm or fuzzy feelings about these unusual-looking creatures, maybe you will be convinced about their usefulness when you consider that frogs eat huge amounts of bugs, including slugs, beetles, cutworms, flies, grasshoppers, moths, sow bugs, pill bugs, centipedes, millipedes, crickets, ants, and earwigs.

As many of the genes and hormones regulating frog reproduction, development, and metabolism perform similar functions in humans, frogs are used as a means to test the impact of exposure to chemicals or other potential toxins. For example, a study on tadpoles to

A red-legged frog. Their permeable skin makes frogs very susceptible to environmental toxins.

examine the impact of a particular pesticide found that the male tadpoles exposed to the pesticide, even at low levels, had significant abnormalities in their reproductive organs. They were losing their male reproductive organs. Some were even growing female organs. This was the case even where the frog's exposure to the pesticide was significantly lower than that deemed safe for humans in drinking water. This raised an alarm about whether this pesticide could play an indirect role in causing cancer.[14]

Perhaps most importantly, however, is the fact that frogs are almost universally accepted as "indicator species" for the health of the environment. With their sensitive skin reacting to the environment, frogs serve as a useful indicator or warning when things are going wrong. This is especially true because frogs live both in water and on land and can act as an early warning, signaling changes or problems in both environments.

Many kids get their first exposure to wildlife through their interactions with frogs.

The fact that we have seen a serious decline in frog populations over the last twenty-five years should be cause for concern. The Global Amphibian Assessment (GAA), a three-year worldwide study by the IUCN released in 2004, found that 32 percent of known amphibians are

Kids to the Rescue

To help the plight of the endangered frogs of Monteverde, a nine-year-old Swedish boy decided that kids could make a difference. Based on his idea, his class raised money to buy chunks of rain forest property in Costa Rica. From bake sales to sing-a-thons, they raised enough funds to buy six hectares (fifteen acres) of land in Monteverde, creating the Children's Eternal Rain Forest. Since then, additional property has been purchased and is owned and operated by the Monteverde Conservation League.[15]

This successful initiative was followed by children from forty-four countries, including the United States, Canada, Great Britain, Germany, and Japan, contributing to the ultimate purchase of over fourteen thousand hectares (thirty-five thousand acres) of tropical forest. This protected land was designated the first International Children's Rainforest of Costa Rica in 1990.

globally threatened, with 456 species critically endangered. Overall, the GAA found 42.5 percent of species to be in decline.[16]

What Can You Do?

How can you help save rain forests and the frogs who live in them? Here are five suggestions:

1. Ask your school to buy environmentally friendly paper.

2. Use less paper. Reduce, reuse, and recycle. Cut up used paper, and reuse the back side as notepads.

3. Do a class project to learn more about rain forests, including the plants and animals living there. Write stories or plays, or decorate the classroom, library, or gym to look like a rain forest.

4. Write a letter thanking an organization or company working to protect the rain forest.

5. Have your class check out a world map and highlight places where rain forests still exist.

6

Slow but Steady: Marine Turtles

Do you think of marine turtles as slow, dim-witted, and uninteresting? If so, you are wrong on all counts. They are amazing creatures, and though they have been studied for years, they still remain a mystery with respect to their life cycles and ocean travels.

You probably would not think a turtle might need a lawyer or an embassy, but there are ongoing legal battles in the fight to protect marine turtles.[1] They may not need passports or photo IDs, but a single marine turtle will cross the borders of many countries and swim through thousands of miles of international waters in its lifetime. These world travelers have been cruising the waters for over 100 million years, outliving virtually all their prehistoric earth-mates. Like sharks, they even survived the extinction of the dinosaurs.[2]

Just because they have been tough enough to survive through the ages when many other species have not does not mean they are invulnerable. That hard shell is not enough to protect marine turtles from the threats facing them today. In fact, six out of seven species of marine turtles are endangered, with three being critically endangered.

The Life Cycle of Marine Turtles

The life cycle of marine turtles is still not fully under-stood—and what is known about it is hard to fathom.

A loggerhead sea turtle hatchling

Turtle Trivia

✳ Pacific leatherbacks are considered the most endangered turtle population, with a drop in the last two decades from ninety thousand leatherbacks in the eastern Pacific alone to an estimated three thousand nesting females remaining.[3]

✳ The largest leatherback ever recorded was an enormous male, found stranded on a beach in Wales in 1988, measuring over two and a half meters (eight feet) long and weighing in at 916 kilograms (2,019 pounds).[4]

✳ In the late 1940s, more than forty thousand nesting Kemp's Ridley turtles came ashore in a single day, as compared to only a few hundred in the late 1980s.[5]

✳ According to the World Wildlife Fund:

> Loggerhead turtles carry veritable animal and plant cities on their shell. As many as 100 species of animals and plants have been recorded living on one single loggerhead turtle.[6]

Seven Marine Turtle Species

* Leatherback
* Hawksbill
* Kemp's Ridley
* Loggerhead
* Olive Ridley
* Green
* Flatback

They are among the few creatures that depend on both land and ocean. They depend on land for reproduction. After traveling hundreds or even thousands of miles, a female turtle will come back to her birthplace, crawl ashore, dig a nest, and lay her eggs on a sandy beach.

No one is sure where turtles go after they "leave home" or how they find their way back. However, one study seemed to indicate that turtles use a simple navigation system involving the earth's magnetic field. This allows the turtles to return to the same egg-laying site. The navigation system acts like a compass, pointing the turtles "home."[7]

The heat of the sand incubates the eggs, and they are able to develop on their own. About two months later, the little hatchlings pop out from the nest and scurry to the water, swimming to reach open ocean currents where they will find food and shelter from land-based predators. Hatchlings face many dangers, and as few as one in one thousand eggs survives to adulthood.[8]

Threats to Marine Turtles

Marine turtles face an increasing number of threats.

Habitat destruction. The most obvious form of habitat destruction is the direct impact of development, where critical nesting beaches literally disappear. Imagine the poor adult female turtle who travels many miles to return home to nest, only to find her nesting site gone and a huge condominium complex in its place.

But there are other less obvious but equally destructive forms of habitat destruction that threaten turtle popula-tions. You may wonder how baby turtles know to dart toward the water as soon as they hatch. Normally, the moon and stars reflect off the water, making the water the brightest light on a night beach. Hatchlings are drawn to this light. But with human development comes lights from roads and

Sea turtles have been cruising the waters for over 100 million years, outliving virtually all their prehistoric earth-mates.

buildings, which attract the hatchlings instead of nature's intended light. In confusion, they are lured away from the water, where they fall victim to predators, starve, or die from the sun's heat the following day.

With development also come seawalls, changing drift patterns and causing erosion or destruction of beaches. Those pristine holiday beaches we enjoy have generally been dredged and filled with sand, destroying important feeding grounds and nesting areas. Similarly, development brings vehicle traffic on beaches, compacting the sand and making it impossible for female turtles to dig their nests.

Coral reefs and sea grass beds are important marine turtle feeding habitats. Tourist development, nutrient runoff, sedimentation, and climate change are only a few culprits responsible for damaging these feeding habitats.

Climate change. An interesting but little-known fact is that the sex of a marine turtle is dependent on the temperature of the developing egg. Not surprisingly, therefore, global warming will change the ratio of male to female turtles and destabilize the population.[9]

Climate change has also been blamed for an increase in nest loss as a result of the increase in tropical storms and erosion of nesting beaches from rising seawater levels. The impact on coral reefs has ripple effects for the marine turtle population, which is dependent on these important feeding habitats.

Volunteers collect Kemp's Ridley sea turtle eggs in an effort to save them from predators.

Bycatch. One of the main causes of marine turtle mortality is destructive fishing techniques, such as the use of gill nets and long-line fishing. Even though they are not the intended target, hundreds of thousands of marine turtles are caught and killed every year in trawls, on long-line hooks, in fishing nets, or in shrimp traps. These unintended catches are called bycatch. As reptiles, marine turtles have lungs. When they cannot reach the surface to breathe, they drown.

Take and trade. Hunting and egg collection have been responsible for drastic declines in populations worldwide. In some countries, marine turtle eggs are considered an aphrodisiac (a food that arouses sexual desire), which makes them popular to poach. Some are sought after for their carapace plates, which are manufactured into tortoiseshell items. Others are killed for leather production. In some countries, young marine turtles are caught, killed, stuffed, and sold as souvenirs.[10]

Human hands are behind a rising number of turtles meeting their death each year—whether for their meat, eggs, shells, or calipee (the green body fat serving as the main ingredient in turtle soup).

Pollution. Pollution can detrimentally affect turtle populations in expected and unexpected ways. Oil spills or other contamination causes obvious damage to marine turtles. Because turtles can live up to one hundred years, pollutants can have a very long-term cumulative impact, building up in the turtles' bodies over years and being passed on to their eggs.[11]

We often do not think of the potential impact our discarded rubbish can have on wildlife. For example, marine turtles can confuse pieces of floating plastic, such as party balloons and plastic shopping bags, for jellyfish. The plastic items can choke the turtles to death when they try to eat them or can get caught in their digestive tracts, causing them to starve. Our careless littering can be responsible for the death of these magnificent creatures.

Similarly, discarded fishing gear can entangle marine turtles, drowning them or leaving them unable to swim or eat.

Boating collisions. Even the hard shell of a marine turtle cannot stand up to the force of a collision with a boat or the slice of a powerful motorboat propeller. The impact from these accidental encounters can seriously damage the shell, leaving the turtle vulnerable. Even worse, the collisions sometimes kill the turtle.[12]

Invasive predators. The introduction of new predators has serious impact on the already precarious chances of young turtle hatchlings. Human development brings garbage. With garbage come raccoons. The dramatic increase in raccoon populations has been devastating for marine turtles, as the raccoons dig up and destroy huge numbers of turtle nests.[13]

Disease. We are seeing an increase in the reports of fatal diseases to marine turtles. Some believe that marine pollution and land runoff may weaken turtles' immune systems, rendering them more susceptible to disease.[14] As noted above, the cumulative impact of toxins and pollutants also plays a role.

Why Should You Care?

Other than the fact that marine turtles have been around for over 100 million years and it would be tragic to see their demise, marine turtles are key species in the ecosystems they inhabit. They help keep balance between rival species. For example, we considered the importance of coral reefs in Chapter 2. Hawksbill turtles eat sponges that aggressively compete with corals for space on the reef. Without this control, sponges would increase and coral reefs would decline, and with them the millions of species who depend on them.

Similarly, sea grass beds are important productive ecosystems, acting as nurseries for many species of invertebrates and fish. Green turtles help maintain these beds and increase their productivity, not to mention that the digested sea grass consumed by turtles then becomes

A green sea turtle off the island of Saipan in the western Pacific Ocean. Climate change and marine pollution threaten turtle habitats the world over.

nutrients to the many plant and animal species living in the sea grass ecosystem.

As predators, turtles help keep prey populations in check. On the flip side, young turtles serve as food for other fish and birds. The disappearance of this important link in the food chain could have profound impact on the marine ecosystem.

Marine turtles have recently become an important ecotourism attraction. People are coming to watch the laying of the eggs. In turn, this helps raise the profile of the issue of larger conservation efforts. That is why marine turtles are considered a flagship species; as an ecotourism attraction, they attract help to themselves as well as the many species with which they coexist, not to mention the broader issue of conservation efforts generally. Tourists also bring significant amounts of money to ecotourism areas and are an important source of income for local communities.[15]

Some females do not breed until they are several decades old, and then they may only produce young every other year or less. With hatchlings and young turtles at increased risk, if they cannot survive long enough to mate, turtle populations will not be able to recover.[16]

What Can You Do?

Consider the steps you can take to help the plight of marine turtles:

Slow but Steady: Marine Turtles

* Do not buy marine turtle products, and push for the prohibition of their sale.

* When you travel, help clean marine turtle nesting beaches to give hatchlings a fighting chance to make it to the water. Get rid of garbage that may be carried out to the water and harm marine turtles.

* At home, make sure you properly dispose of garbage so that it will not end up in water where it can have an impact on endangered species.

* Write to decision makers about the plight of marine turtles and other endangered animals. You can either compose the letters and choose the recipients yourself, or you can participate in organized letter-writing campaigns.

* Educate others; talk to family and friends about the plight of marine turtles. Do you have to write a speech for school? Consider doing it on marine turtles. Try to encourage others to support conservation efforts.

7

Wolves: I'll Huff and I'll Puff

Whether they are huffing and puffing to eat little pigs or dressing up as Grandma to eat little girls, wolves have traditionally gotten a bad rap. Folklore and popular culture play a significant role in how society views a particular animal species. Usually cast as the villain in children's stories, wolves have inspired fear for generations. Just take the seemingly harmless story of the *Three Little Pigs* as an example. The wolf is portrayed as a heartless, bloodthirsty creature, willing to destroy house and home in order to find his next meal. Such stories may be the first exposure to wolves for many children. But does the fiction reflect reality? Are wolves really vicious killing machines?

The reality is that wolves are naturally curious, playful creatures, with a social structure probably paralleling that

The wolf´s reputation as a vicious killer is not deserved.

of humans more closely than most animals. Ironically, it was the introduction of humans, as pioneers began to settle North America, that upset the natural balance and forced wolves to prey on livestock. In response, humans sought to exterminate the species, driving wolves to the brink of extinction. Only recently, with the advent of movies and stories purportedly told from the wolf's perspective, are we starting to see the stereotype debunked in popular culture.

There is now a strong lobby for the conservation of wolves, recognizing that in addition to their natural beauty and interesting social patterns, wolves are key to the forest ecosystem food chain, acting as top-down predators, keeping populations in check and the ecosystem in balance.

How Did Wolves Get Such a Bad Rap?

The indigenous people of North America admired the wolf. In fact, it was considered desirable to emulate, or copy, this impressive canine creature. American Indians had a profound respect for their brother, the wolf. They honored its hunting abilities and perceived wolves as wise, powerful teachers. Some strategies they used in hunting big game, such as buffalo or caribou, were learned from the wolves.

So how did settling European pioneers come to fear and revile the wolf? Though the age of enlightenment was approaching, superstition still abounded in the Middle Ages in Europe. People believed in werewolves. They believed wolves were a danger to humans. It is said that the Church exploited this fear and used it to maintain secular control. It is not surprising that European settlers landing in America carried deeply held sinister images of the wolf with them.

It did not help that as pioneers settled in North America, the wolves' natural prey began to be wiped out. As humans developed wolf habitats through rapid forest logging and land clearing, they also hunted prey that used to be the wolves' domain. Deer and elk populations were depleted, and bison were almost completely annihilated. Out of necessity, as wolves' food sources dwindled, they began to prey on livestock. This fed the preexisting human fear and distrust of wolves.

What was the pioneers' reaction? They began a course of intentional destruction of wolves. Bounties were offered—money for bringing in dead wolves. Between 1850 and 1900 significant numbers were killed. In 1907, settlers and the federal government called for the total extinction of the species, and the wolf population was nearly eliminated. By the 1930s, over 95 percent of the wolf population had been destroyed by means of poison, guns, traps, or other human persecution.[1]

"Wolves were hunted and killed with more passion than any other animal in U.S. history," according to the

U.S. Fish and Wildlife Service (USFWS).[2] Unfortunately, as so often seems to be the case through human history, when we fear something, rather than seeking to understand it, we react by trying to destroy it. The problem is compounded, because humans historically view themselves as the dominant species, believing we have an inherent right to eliminate other species we deem a problem.

It is clear wolves were not understood. Beliefs about this majestic animal were extreme, from cultures who revered the wolves as gods or those, like the pioneers, who reviled them as devils. Either way, as noted by one wolf conservationist, "the wolf has often paid with its life for crimes it did not commit."[3]

About Wolves

How do we go about debunking the negative stereotype? Knowledge is the first step. It is important to learn the reality about wolves, rather than the myths. Wolves are intelligent, playful, social creatures.

Have you ever seen a dog drop his front quarters into a crouch, tail wagging to signal that it is playtime? Well, wolves do the same. They love to play. Play fights and chases are favorites as they wrestle each other to the ground, throwing their forepaws around each other's necks.

Little Red Riding Hood is stalked by a slavering wolf. Stories and superstitions about wolves have persisted in some cultures, creating unfounded fear of the animals.

"All the better to eat you with, my dear." Wolves smile, open mouthed, showing their teeth. With twelve incisors, four canines, sixteen premolars, and ten carnassials and molars, it can seem quite intimidating—especially considering that the canine teeth are one-inch long, strong, sharp, and slightly curved to grasp prey.

When wolves play, or when they are reestablishing the pack hierarchy, they often appear to bite each other's necks or muzzles. It can look fearsome, so it is no wonder observers view the wolf as aggressive and dangerous, but the reality is that it is merely part of their natural routine and rarely leads to physical harm.

If the wolf intended to hurt, it could easily do so. The wolf has very strong jaws; it is believed that a wolf jaw's crushing pressure is double that of a German shepherd's. Their strong jaws allow wolves to crush bones to get to the soft marrow. Wolves do not have the best table manners; they do not chew their food, but they scissor off pieces of meat to swallow in manageable chunks.

While wolves may not have great table manners, they are well groomed. They wash themselves in rivers and streams, and they also lick each other's coats, nibbling to remove foreign matter. This reciprocal grooming is believed to strengthen social bonds and is especially prevalent during courtship, or mating, rituals.

Wolves: I'll Huff and I'll Puff

"All the better to see you with, my dear." Wolves have keen eyesight, quick to detect even slight movements, even though their eyes are in front, allowing only one hundred and eighty-degree vision (unlike some of their prey species, which can see over three hundred degrees). Wolves also have keen hearing, able to hear up to 9.7 kilometers (six miles) away in forest conditions and 16 kilometers (ten miles) in the open. Consider how far away your school or the local mall is from home. Now imagine being able to easily hear conversations from there while standing in your driveway. That could be a useful skill!

It is not surprising that wolves also have a highly developed sense of smell. In fact, scent plays an important role in a wolf's life. Wolves can locate prey by smell alone, but they can also use this skill to locate other pack members or enemies. Through scent, wolves can tell if other wolves have been in their territory, whether they were male or female, and how recent the visit was. Each wolf has specialized glands; the scent from these glands is individual or unique to each wolf, much like our fingerprints. These scent glands are used to mark boundaries and trails.

Walk a mile in my shoes. Wolves, like their brothers in the canine family, walk on their toe tips, the heel of their feet not coming in contact with the ground. For greater weight distribution and greater support, the wolf's front feet are exceptionally large. These front feet have five toes, but only four are used. The fifth toe has actually regressed to the middle of the foot; it is called the dewclaw. The hind feet have only four toes each. Some scientists believe the human "baby toe" is similarly regressing.

The claws are strong, but blunt, worn off by constant contact with the ground. The claws are not used to attack prey, but rather for digging and gripping the earth while running. Wolves need all the grip they can get as they reach speeds of up to sixty-four kilometers (forty miles) per hour. Believe it or not, they can keep up this speed for several kilometers.

Talk to me. How do wolves communicate? In addition to the scent marking noted above, wolves are famous for their howls—eyes closed, head tilted, sending their mournful sound out into the night air. Howling is a primary means of communication for wolves for everything from keeping in touch through forested areas or over long distances, summoning pack members to a particular location, declaring territory, or for communal, social reasons.

Group sessions are something like our choirs, with wolves howling at different tones and pitches. The group howl can serve as a warning to other packs or to celebrate. Before a hunt, wolves can be seen howling,

Wolves communicate a variety of messages through howling.

hugging, and pressing against each other. Wolves will howl for sheer joy, but also for loneliness. This latter type of howl is sometimes associated with searching for a mate. Researchers have discovered that wolves will even answer humans when we imitate their howls.

In addition to scents and howls, wolves, like humans, communicate through body posture. The signs can be subtle or obvious, but all serve to communicate.

We often hear the expression "a lone wolf" and use it to describe people who are standoffish or loners. In fact, lone wolves are the exception to the rule. Wolves generally belong to family groups, called packs. Within these family packs, there is a definite social structure. There is typically a male parent, a female parent, their pups, and a few other adult wolves who are older brothers and sisters. The pack works together to hunt and care for the pups. The alpha male and female parents are the leaders. In larger packs, there is usually also a beta wolf, or second in command. One wolf, the lowest-ranking wolf, assumes the role of omega, the baby-sitter. The omega is dominated by the other wolves in the pack, including those subordinate to the alphas.

Although they look vicious when they "fight" for rank, the reality is that order is established and maintained through posturing and ritualized fights or bluffing. One wolf conservationist says, "wolves prefer psychological warfare to physical confrontations, meaning that

Body Language

Here are a few examples of body language used by wolves:

* Dominance: Dominant wolves stand stiff legged, with ears erect and forward and hackles slightly bristled. The tail is often held vertical and curled toward the back. This body posture reinforces the wolf's rank to others in the pack.

* Submission: The submissive wolf will lower its entire body, with lips and ears drawn back. The tail is down or between the legs, with the back partially arched. In more extreme cases, the wolf will actually roll on its back and expose its throat and underside to the dominant wolf. The wolf may draw its paws into its body and whine.

* Fear: Frightened wolves try to make themselves look smaller and less conspicuous. They flatten their ears down against their head, tail tucked between the legs, much like submissive wolf posture.

* Happiness: Like a dog, a happy wolf will wag its tail. When it wants to play, it will wag its tail and bow, placing the front of its body low to the ground.

* Aggression: The lips may curl up or pull back, ears erect. An aggressive wolf will snarl and bristle its fur. It may crouch, ready to attack.

high-ranking status is based more on personality or attitude than on size or physical strength."[4] That sounds like many human social relations, probably even the dynamic of some of the relationships at your school. It is often said that attitude is everything. The wolf community is no exception. The alpha male is not necessarily the largest, or even the strongest physically, but is inevitably the one with the strongest personality and attitude.

All the wolves in a pack take care of and raise the pups. The pups are dependent on the mother and other pack members at the outset, as they are born blind and deaf. They are vulnerable and may fall prey to golden eagles or bears. Adult wolves are known to decoy bears away from the pup's den to keep the pups safe. But pups can also die from disease, malnutrition, or starvation.

Wolves have been known to bury the dead pups. In fact, according to R. D. Lawrence, who is famous for his studies while living with wolves, "when any puppies are lost, wolves mourn as deeply as might a human family faced by similar tragedies."[5]

Current Risks or Threats

Are wolves still at risk? They once roamed throughout North America, but since being driven to the brink of extinction they have now been reduced to 3 percent of their former range in the United States outside Alaska.[6] The Federal Endangered Species Act of 1973 listed all populations of the subspecies in the United States as endangered. Since that time there has been an increase in wolf populations in certain areas, and the status of wolves has been downgraded from endangered to threatened.

Classifying the status of animals is a judgment call that can be complex. There is currently disagreement and much debate about whether wolves ought to continue to be classified as endangered.

Those in favor of ongoing protection cite the fact that the gray wolf only occupies a tiny fraction of its former range in the contiguous forty-eight states and that most of the habitat in these states is currently unsuitable for wolves, due largely to human encroachment. Further, the habitat problem is only likely to get worse as trends in land use suggest that potential wolf habitats will continue to be developed and rendered similarly unsuitable for wolves. They point out that wolves were practically exterminated, and that it was only after wolves were given protection by the Endangered Species Act that wolf populations in the United States began to increase. If wolves' protected status is removed, the concern is that they will be persecuted again, as public attitudes are mixed, with strong antiwolf sentiment still a problem.

Those arguing against protected status rely on viable populations in Alaska, Canada, and other nations worldwide, suggesting that protection in the forty-eight

U.S. contiguous states is therefore unnecessary. They also point to the significant cost to the federal government for its control program under the Endangered Species Act. They suggest this money could better be used to save other, more endangered species.

The debate really heated up when gray wolves were slated to be removed from the endangered species list for the northern Rocky Mountains recently. The proposal from the U.S. Fish and Wildlife Service originated in 2007, and the period for comments from the public ran until the end of November 2008. Some people thought the delisting ruling should be cause for celebration. Surely the removal of wolves from the list meant they had been successfully reintroduced and managed. But wolf conservationists were not popping any champagne corks at the news. In fact, they stepped to the plate and initiated a flurry of legal action to stop the USFWS from removing wolves from the endangered list.

> If wolves' protected status is removed, the concern is that they will be persecuted again.

Why were they so opposed to the proposal? The ruling would have turned wolf management over to state and tribal agencies that plan to actively reduce wolf populations. These state management plans would allow trophy hunting and trapping of wolves as well as lethal control (legal killing) of wolves harming livestock or eating "too many" deer and elk. With wolves classified as predatory animals, they could be killed without hunting licenses, even in "wolf-killing contests." The plans only required the states of Idaho, Montana, and Wyoming to each maintain wolf populations of one hundred, with ten breeding pairs. Conservationists believe that number is not enough to protect wolf populations. Evolutionary biologist Robert Wayne said the plan "severely underestimates the number of wolves required for maintaining a genetically healthy, self-sustaining meta-population."[7] Wildlife biologist Carlos Carroll says, "New data suggests that several thousand wolves may be needed before delisting should be considered."[8]

Since May 2009, the gray wolf has been removed from the endangered species list in all areas except for Wyoming. The debate is likely not over, and the fate of the wolves will hang in the balance as the competing interest groups continue to try to gain ground.

Unfortunately, as humans posed the largest single threat to wolves during the period of persecution, even with protected status today, it seems humans continue to pose the greatest survival threat to wolves. Humans continue to encroach into wolf territory, even as studies consistently show a causal connection to the demise of wolves, who need open land and abundant prey.

According to experts at the Natural Resources Research Institute, "human contact has historically been the major source of wolf mortality. Human contact has meant high levels of legal, illegal, and accidental killing of wolves."[9]

Humans also have an indirect negative impact on wolves. As humans develop wolf habitat, prey populations necessary to the wolves' survival are depleted, leading to starvation. Development also brings increased highway traffic, causing a rise in wolf mortality from car accidents. Similarly, disease and parasites, which are higher in more developed areas, pose a threat to both reproductive abilities of wolves and pup survival.[10]

Why Should We Care?

Conservationists who have lived with and studied wolves have come away profoundly moved and changed by the experience. They have invariably developed strong bonds with the wolves in their study pack, knowing them, with their individual personalities, as one would know their own family members. The social structure of wolves is much like our human family network. Some go so far as to suggest that wolves are a reflection of mankind. "Either we accept the wolf as an essential part of our nature, or we will follow him . . . into decline," says Dr. Erik Zimen.[11]

R. D. Lawrence also spoke to this experience:

Wolves: I'll Huff and I'll Puff

Anyone who has had a close relationship with wolves can never forget them. In some unexplainable way, these animals are able to give to their human friends an awareness and an understanding of life that was missing before the relationship. Perhaps this is because wolves are so extraordinarily perceptive and so joyfully eager to appraise and understand all the influences that surround them at all times. . . . Day by day, wolves teach their human friends by their own examples.[12]

Wolves also play a critical role as a controlling factor in forest food chains. As top predators, wolves keep deer and elk populations in check. When overpopulation of deer and elk occur, the results wreak havoc on the food chain. Natural ecosystems are adversely affected as deer affect the growth and survival of herbs, shrubs, and tree species, which then has ripple effects on insects, birds, and other mammals. Overbrowsing of tree seedlings by an overabundant deer population reduces species diversity in forests, reduces tree growth, and ultimately results in reduced protection from erosion and floods.

In their natural habitat, wolves serve as subjects for scientists to study, a natural laboratory of sorts. In fact, according to University of California professor Michael Soule, "the most trenchant message from conservation science in the last decade comes from studies about the role of top predators in maintaining the health of ecosystems."[13]

All the members of a wolf pack help take care of the pups.

In addition to the impact on the ecosystem, studies of deer overabundance have shown resulting major economic losses in forestry, agriculture, and transportation as well as transmission of disease. Trees browsed by deer decrease in commercial value and can actually die. Similarly, agricultural crops are damaged by deer to the tune of many millions of dollars in the United States alone.[14] Also consider the cost, both financial and in terms of human life, as deer overabundance increase vehicle accident rates.

Increased deer populations also increase transmission of tick-borne diseases, some of which threaten human health. Similarly, risk of bovine tuberculosis, causing mortality in livestock, other wildlife, and humans, is increased, as is chronic wasting disease, similar to "mad cow" disease.

While deer are amazing creatures in their own right, the studies about the impact of their overabundance reinforces the importance of ensuring ecological balance of all species in nature. As a keystone species and as top predators, wolves help facilitate this role.

What Can We Do?

What is in store for the future? Humans have to come to understand the adverse impact we have on nature when we interfere with its innate balance. As human impacts increase, we need to focus on restoring the balance that has been upset. Applying this theory to wolves, it will not be enough to protect the current numbers or to set minimum number thresholds. It is necessary to restore the species to areas from which we have extirpated, or totally uprooted, them. To protect the wolves, we need to protect their habitats to the extent still possible.

A delicate balancing of competing interests is required, as wolves need large areas with little human contact to ensure viable populations. This need obviously conflicts with existing land uses, such as

Recently, the status of wolves in the United States has been changed from endangered to threatened. Debates continue over how wolf populations should be classified.

human developments and livestock production. But if we are serious about ensuring recovery for wolf populations, we need to look at expanding potential habitats and ensuring large enough populations that the species will be more resilient.

The debate over recovery goals for wolves "illuminates a larger debate over the necessity for rewilding, a reversal of the trend toward increasing human domination of Earth's natural ecosystems," according to a joint study funded in part by the Turner Endangered Species Fund.[15] How do we achieve this?

Wolves: I'll Huff and I'll Puff

A cross-boundary, multiagency coordination will be necessary to successfully manage wolf populations. We need to ensure open corridors for wolves to travel between states and countries. Interest groups need to work together to find feasible compromises that will be respected and enforced.

Wolves are undomesticated—intended to live in free open spaces. When humans interfere in the natural order of things, does it then become our responsibility to try to balance the upset we cause? Arguably it is our responsibility to ensure a healthy environment for the wolves, since we destroyed their habitat with our arrival and persecuted them for it.

We must find a way to live with these unique social carnivores who so resemble us. Through fear and ignorance, humans almost exterminated the entire wolf population. Do we now owe it to them and ourselves to reverse that pattern? Can we find a way to live side by side with these magnificent creatures? Will we protect the songs of the wolves? Will we join them in song? The next full moon, consider going outside and howling, calling on our brother the wolf. You never know—you just might get an answer.

8

Sharks: Predators or Prey?

A sleek, torpedo-shaped, silver-gray shark cleanly slices through the water. Multiple rows of jagged teeth line his jaws. Does that conjure up images of a vicious killing machine? Sharks are often portrayed in the media as terrifying predators—a dangerous threat to humans. But are they? The truth is that humans are now the greatest threat to sharks.

We hear about sensational shark attacks, but the reality is that more people are killed by dogs, deer, lightning, falling coconuts, and even vending machines than by sharks.[1] By contrast, through overfishing and shark finning, humans are depleting worldwide shark populations at an alarming rate. Over 100 million sharks are killed each year for their fins alone.[2] We are seeing an unprecedented devastation of shark populations around the world.

Jaws: Source of the Problem?

The movie *Jaws* may be the primary reason that most people are afraid of sharks. The movie, which tells the story of a great white shark tormenting a small seaside community, is based on the best-selling book by Peter Benchley. The film made almost $130 million in the United States alone and made sharks public enemy number one.[3]

Why Should You Care?

Admittedly, sharks are not cuddly or lovable. But they are an important part of the marine ecosystem. We need healthy oceans. To remain healthy, marine ecosystems need to stay in balance. Sharks, as top predators in the ocean, are a key component in marine food chains. Many believe that sharks have even shaped the evolution of ocean species. Marine life has been forced to adapt to protect against their natural predators. These adaptations include schooling behavior, camouflage, speed, size, and communications. Scientists also believe that sharks play a key role in marine ecosystems by keeping prey populations in check.[4] While the environmental impact of depleting shark populations from ocean ecosystems

The scary appearance of the shark has contributed to its
reputation as a killing machine.

is complex, it is widely believed that removing this control is likely to have a damaging effect on marine ecosystems.

Sharks have been a vital part of ocean life for 400 million years. They were here 200 million years before the dinosaurs.[5] Yet now, many species of shark are at risk. Most sharks grow slowly, mature late, have a long gestation period, and give birth to only a few large pups. So once depleted, the shark population recovers slowly, if at all. Shark finning, long-lining, and overfishing are key human threats.

Shark Finning

Shark finning is the practice of cutting the fins off captured sharks and discarding the rest of the animal at sea. The sharks are often still alive when their fins are cut off and their bodies thrown back into the water.[6] Imagine the horrible pain they must suffer as they fall to

Ancient Animals

Sharks are among the earth's oldest animals. The ancestors of the modern shark date back to over 400 million years ago. Surprisingly, shark species have changed relatively little during that time span, earning them the nickname "living fossils."[7]

A white-tipped reef shark. The top predators in the ocean, sharks are believed to have shaped the evolution of ocean species.

the ocean floor, bleeding to death and unable to swim. What does it say about humans as a species that we can treat another living creature with such cruelty and so little respect? Aside from the moral problems with this practice, how can we justify wasting 95 percent of the animal when people are starving around the world? Think of the number of people who could be fed from the meat left to rot at the bottom of the ocean.

Known in China as *yu chi* or "fish wings," shark fins can sell for U.S. $400 per kilogram (U.S. $880 per pound) or more, making them extremely financially lucrative. People pay large amounts of money for a bowl of shark fin soup, which is found widely in Asia. Shark fin soup is even on the menu at Hong Kong Disneyland.[8] It is considered a sign of prestige and is a traditional means of honoring special guests or occasions. The irony is that shark fins are tasteless, so chefs actually have to add pork or chicken for flavor![9]

The increase in demand for shark fin soup has made shark finning attractive as it allows for easy profit. Because the practice takes place at sea, fishermen only have to carry the fins. There is no need for storage or refrigeration. It is now a multibillion-dollar industry.[10]

Long-lining

Long-lining is a practice that further threatens shark populations. Fishing fleets, targeting valuable fish such as tuna, will lay out miles of fishing line (longlines) with thousands of baited hooks. It is estimated that 10 billion longline hooks are set out worldwide each year.[11] These lines, however, invariably catch considerably more unintended species, or bycatch, than the targeted fish. In fact, the National Coalition for Marine Conservation suggests that only 1–2 percent of fish caught are actually the targeted species. In other words, for every one hundred hooks with catches, ninety-eight or ninety-nine unintended marine animals are caught.[12]

In addition to the unintended deaths of seabirds, sea turtles, and other marine mammals, this bycatch usually includes significant numbers of sharks. While shark bycatch used to be considered a nuisance, and the sharks were cut loose and allowed to swim away (if still alive), as shark fins have become more valuable, sharks are being finned and their carcasses discarded.[13] This is true regardless of the shark's age, size, or species. Some are too small to be taken legally at all.

> **Sharks have been a vital part of ocean life for 400 million years.**

This bycatch is often not reported. Therefore it is difficult to even get accurate data on the extent of the shark depletion problem.[14] However, experts estimate that numerous species of sharks will be lost altogether within the next decade if the practice of long-lining is not controlled. Some Atlantic shark populations have declined by as much as 80 percent.[15]

Overfishing

Threats to shark population and the stability of the marine ecosystem also threaten traditional local sustainable fisheries. This is particularly so as large industrial foreign fishing vessels invade local waters around the world.

Consider recent changes in fishing methods: fish-finding sonar, satellite locating systems, longlines with thousands of hooks, massive nets, spotter helicopters,

A shark boat in South Carolina. Despite evidence of overfishing and species depletion, few countries restrict shark fishing.

and factory ships that operate around the clock. With all this technology, many fish have nowhere left to hide.[16] Plus, few countries restrict shark fishing despite growing evidence of overfishing and depletion. There are virtually no international limits on the catch of sharks. It is not illegal to sell shark fin soup or other shark products.[17] The export of products doubled in the last decade, and the demand for shark fin soup is estimated to be increasing by 5 percent per year.[18]

What Can You Do?

Few people fight to save the sharks. It is not as trendy or high profile as campaigns to save more lovable wildlife like the panda. But despite their terrifying image, the simple fact is that sharks are vulnerable.

Most experts agree that the simplest, most effective way to implement a shark-finning ban is to require that sharks are landed whole with fins still attached. This requirement would also improve the collection of data necessary for assessing shark population status, because more accurate and reliable records of species and number of sharks killed could be obtained.

You can help by signing a petition, writing a letter asking for a worldwide ban on shark finning, informing others about the problem, and avoiding eating shark fin soup. But the first step is changing the way we look at sharks. They deserve our respect, not our fear.

9

And the Verdict Is ...?

Now you have had a chance to explore and consider these underappreciated creatures. Do you think they are misunderstood? Are they more valuable than you had originally given them credit for? Will you look at them in the same way now? Whether you love them, hate them, or something in between, do you think they are worth protecting? What is your verdict?

These seemingly different animals all share some common characteristics or attributes. They all are suffering serious population decline, all are at risk, and all play a vital role in our ecosystem. The disappearance of any one of these animal species would upset nature's precarious balance and have serious ripple effects, not the least of which would be a profound impact on humans. Some would say our very survival is at stake.

The disappearance of even one species, such as this Indiana bat, could have serious effects on the balance of nature.

And the Verdict Is ...?

Interestingly, many of the dangers threatening these animals are the same: habitat destruction, overexploitation, competition with alien species, pollution, and climate change. The primary risks facing these varied species are caused by humans, either directly or indirectly.

So what can we do? What can you do? Sometimes when the implications of a problem seem so serious and huge, it can be overwhelming. There is a tendency to assume there is nothing useful we can achieve, certainly not on our own, and therefore we ignore the problem. But that approach rarely makes sense. Knowledge is power. We have been given warning signs and have an opportunity to make changes. We can take steps to correct the problems and reverse these disturbing trends.

Whether your motivation is out of a sense of duty or responsibility, interest for the animals, recognition of their importance to the ecosystem, desire to ensure our ability to enjoy them (now and for future generations), or whether your motivation is less altruistic, such as concern about their economic value, desire to save our food supply, or self-preservation, clearly there is great benefit to looking for solutions. Solutions can only be reached one step at a time, even if they seem like baby steps in the face of a large and complex problem.

May some of these problems correct themselves over time through the normal course? Will species adapt and change as necessary? Yes, that is possible. But is it likely that all of them will resolve themselves? Is that a chance we want to take? Is that a chance we should take?

You are now aware of the issue. That is one big step forward. It is hoped that these animals, and the larger issue of the need for conservation generally, are now better understood. You may now feel compelled to do your part, taking one important baby step at a time. Spread the word. You can make a difference. As more people come to understand, more people will care. More will speak up, and more will choose to act. Eventually, those baby steps will become a stampede to ensure we are not part of another mass extinction.

Chapter Notes

Chapter 1. Introduction: Unloved and Endangered

1. "Endangered Species," *OECD Glossary of Statistical Terms*, March 4, 2003, <http://stats.oecd.org/glossary/detail.asp?ID=791> (March 31, 2008).
2. "The IUCN Red List of Threatened Species," *International Union for Conservation of Nature and Natural Resources*, 2008, <www.iucnredlist.org/static/categories_criteria> (November 17, 2008).
3. "Endangered Species," *Science Daily*, n.d., <http://www.sciencedaily.com/articles/e/endangered_species.htm> (March 31, 2008).
4. "Current Mass Extinction Period Awareness," n.d., <http://www.butterflycry.com/massextinction.html> (March 31, 2008).
5. Ibid.
6. Monte Hummel, "Environmental and Conservation Movements," *The Canadian Encyclopedia*, 2008, <http://www.thecanadianencyclopedia.com/index.cfm?PgNm=TCE&Params=A1ARTA0002627> (March 31, 2008).
7. Ibid.
8. Sophie Boukhari, "Too Valuable for Price Tags," *UNESCO Courier Journalist*, May 2000, p. 24.
9. Karen McGhee, "The Good Fight," *Australian Geographic*, issue 88, October–December 2007, pp. 104–117.
10. Boukhari, p. 25.

Chapter 2. In Search of Nemo: Coral Reefs

1. John Weier, "Mapping the Decline of Coral Reefs," *Earth Observatory: NASA*, March 12, 2001, <http://earthobservatory.nasa.gov/Study/Coral/> (March 31, 2008).
2. "Corals > Ecology," *World Wildlife Fund*, n.d., <http://worldwildlife.org/coral/ecology.cfm> (February 7, 2008).
3. John Tibbetts, "The State of the Oceans, Part 2: Delving Deeper in the Sea's Bounty," *Environmental Health Perspectives*, vol. 112, no. 8, June 2004, p. A473.
4. "Corals > Ecology".
5. Tibbetts, p. A473.
6. "People and Corals," *Reefs At Risk*, Australian Institute of Marine Sciences, n.d., <http://www3.aims.gov.au/pages/research/project-net/reefs-at-risk/apnet-rar03.html> (December 8, 2008).

7. "The Living Reef," *Reefs At Risk*, Australian Institute of Marine Sciences, n.d., <http://www3.aims.gov.au/pages/research/project-net/reefs-at-risk/apnet-rar02.html> (December 8, 2008).
8. "People and Corals."
9. Tibbetts, p. A475.
10. Ibid.
11. "The Living Reef."
12. Tibbetts, p. A473.
13. "The Threats and the Causes," *Reefs At Risk*, Australian Institute of Marine Sciences, n.d., <http://www3.aims.gov.au/pages/research/project-net/reefs-at-risk/apnet-rar04.html> (December 8, 2008).
14. Ibid.
15. Ibid.
16. "The Effects of Climate Change," *Reefs At Risk*, Australian Institute of Marine Sciences, n.d., <http://www3.aims.gov.au/pages/research/project-net/reefs-at-risk/apnet-rar05.html> (December 8, 2008).
17. "The Threats and the Causes."
18. "A World-Wide Threat of Ecological Collapse," *Reefs At Risk*, Australian Institute of Marine Sciences, n.d., <http://www3.aims.gov.au/pages/research/project-net/reefs-at-risk/ apnet-rar01.html> (March 31, 2008).
19. "Managing for Change," *Reefs At Risk*, Australian Institute of Marine Sciences, n.d., <http://www3.aims.gov.au/pages/research/project-net/reefs-at-risk/apnet-rar06.html> (December 8, 2008).
20. "Facing the Challenge," *Reefs At Risk*, Australian Institute of Marine Sciences, n.d., <http://www3.aims.gov.au/pages/research/project-net/reefs-at-risk/apnet-rar08.html> (December 8, 2008).

Chapter 3. Bees—What's the Buzz?

1. David M. Schwartz, "Birds, Bees and Even Nectar Feeding Bats Do It," *Smithsonian*, vol. 31, issue 1, April 2000, pp. 58–67.
2. Maureen Dolan, "The Buzz about Bees: A Flush Fund of Fascinating Facts," *Tales from the Hive, NOVA*, n.d., <http://www.pbs.org/wgbh/nova/bees/buzz.html> (April 4, 2008).
3. Schwartz, pp. 58–67.
4. Ibid.
5. Douglas McInnis, "The Plight of the Bumblebee," *Popular Science*, vol. 251, issue 5, November 1997, pp. 78–83.
6. Schwartz, pp. 58–67.
7. David Stipp, "Flight of the Honeybee," *Fortune*, vol. 156, issue 5, March 9, 2007, pp. 108–116.

8. "Declining Bee Numbers Raise Concerns Over Plant Pollination," *ScienceDaily*, May 11, 2007, <http://www.sciencedaily.com/releases/2007/05/070510114621.htm> (December 9, 2008).

9. "Status of Pollinators in North America," *The National Academy of Sciences*, n.d., <http://dels.nas.edu/dels/rpt_briefs/pollinators_brief_final.pdf> (March 31, 2008).

10. Daniel Imhoff, "A Plea for Bees," *Vegetarian Times*, June 2005, p. 82.

11. "Honey Bee Decline Entomologists Buzzing About Vanishing Bee Populations," *ScienceDaily*, July 1, 2007, <http://www.sciencedaily.com/video/2007/0703-honeybee_decline> (February 28, 2008).

12. Stipp, pp. 108–116.

13. "Losing Bees, Butterflies and Other Pollinators," *ScienceDaily*, April 13, 2007, <http://www.sciencedaily.com/releases/2007/04/070409214541.htm> (February 28, 2008).

14. Schwartz, pp. 58–67.

15. "Honey Bee Disappearance (CCD) and What You Can Do," *North American Pollinator Protection Campaign*, n.d., <http://www.nappc.org/NAPPC_Resources/CCD%20Response%20FINAL.pdf> (March 31, 2008).

Chapter 4. I Think I'm Going Batty: Bats

1. "Going Batty! Bats as Pollinators and All-Natural Pest Controllers," n.d., <http://www.pollinator.org/Resources/Going%20BATTY .pdf> (March 31, 2008).

2. Emma Young, "Bat Bites Blamed for US Rabies Deaths," *New Scientist.com*, May 3, 2002, <http://www.newscientist.com/article/dn2243-bat-bites-blamed-for-us-rabies-deaths.html> (April 4, 2008).

3. "Public Health Issues," *Bat Conservation International*, n.d., <http://www.batcon.org/index.php/education/bats-and-the-public/faqs/subcategory/62.html> (December 9, 2008).

4. "Diversity and Distributions," *Bat Conservation International*, n.d., <http://www.batcon.org/index.php/education/article-and-information/natural-history-of-bats/subcategory/15.html> (December 9, 2008).

5. "Common Misconceptions About Bats," *U.S. Fish & Wildlife Service*, n.d., <http://www.fws.gov/endangered/bats/miscon.htm> (February 27, 2008).

6. Ibid.

7. "Going Batty! Bats as Pollinators and All-Natural Pest Controllers."

8. "Reasons for Decline," *U.S. Fish & Wildlife Service*, n.d., <http://www.fws.gov/endangered/bats/threats.htm> (February 27, 2008).

9. Michael Hill, "Bats Dropping like Flies," *Globe and Mail*, January 30, 2008, <http://www.theglobeandmail.com/servlet/story/RTGAM.20080130.wbatsnot0130/BNStory/Science/home> (March 31, 2008).

10. Dan Shapley, "'The Gravest Threat to Bats Ever Seen': White Nose Syndrome Could Quickly Lead to Extinction," *The Daily Green.com*, February 5, 2008, http://www.thedailygreen.com/environmental-news/latest/white-nose-syndrome-bats-47020509 (September 17, 2009).

11. Bob Burtt, "Experts Busy Talking about the Birds and the Bats; Decline in Pollinating Insects and Animals Could Impact Ecosystems, Food Supplies," *Guelph Mercury*, December 13, 2006, p. B1.

12. "Ecological & Economic Value," *Bat Conservation International*, n.d., <http://www.batcon.org/home/index.asp?print=y&idPage=121&idSubPage=55> (March 31, 2008).

13. Ibid.

14. Douglas H. Chadwick, "A Mine of Its Own," *Smithsonian*, May 2004, <http://www.smithsonianmag.com/science-nature/phenom-may-2004.html> (March 31, 2008).

Chapter 5. Someday My Prince Will Come: Frogs

1. "Frogtastic Facts," *Hop To It—Irish Frog Survey*, n.d., <http://www.ipcc.ie/frogfacts.html> (April 4, 2008).

2. "Amphibian Species Lists," *Amphibiaweb*, December 2008, <http://amphibiaweb.org/lists/index.shtml> (December 30, 2008).

3. "Factors Contributing to Declines in Amphibian Population Sizes and Occurrences," *Canadian Amphibian and Reptile Conservation Network*, n.d., <http://www.carcnet.ca/english/amphibians/amphIssues.html> (March 31, 2008).

4. Ibid.

5. "Major Threats," *Global Amphibian Assessment*, May 2006, <http://www.globalamphibians.org/threats.htm> (February 28, 2008).

6. Bridget Wayland, "It's Not Easy Being Green," *Harrowsmith Country Life*, vol. 29, issue 182, June 2005, p. 48.

7. "No Single Reason for Amphibian Decline," *ScienceDaily*, November 19, 1999, <http://www.sciencedaily.com/releases/1999/11/991119075426.htm> (February 28, 2008).

8. Christy Brownlee, "The Case of the Croaking Frogs," *Science World*, April 17, 2006, pp. 14–17.

9. J. Alan Pounds, "Climate and Amphibian Declines," *Nature*, vol. 410, April 5, 2001, pp. 639–640.

10. Ibid.

11. Ibid.

12. Ross A. Alford and Stephen J. Richards, "Global Amphibian Declines: A Problem in Applied Ecology," *Annual Review of Ecology and Systematics*, vol. 30 (1999), pp. 133–165.

13. "Factors Contributing to Declines in Amphibian Population Sizes and Occurrences."

14. William Souder, "It's Not Easy Being Green," *Harper's Magazine*, August 2006, pp. 59-66.

15. Brownlee.

16. "Red List Status," *Global Amphibian Assessment*, n.d., <http://www.globalamphibians.org/assessment.htm> (February 28, 2008).

Chapter 6. **Slow but Steady: Marine Turtles**

1. Chris Wold, "The Status of Sea Turtles under International Environmental Law and International Environmental Agreements," *Journal of International Wildlife Law and Policy*, vol. 5, 2002, pp. 11–48; and J. Frazier, "Marine Turtles and International Instruments: The Agony and the Ecstasy," *Journal of International Wildlife Law and Policy*, vol. 5, 2002, pp. 1–10.

2. "Marine Turtles," *World Wildlife Fund*, n.d., <http://www.world wildlife.org/turtles/> (February 25, 2008).

3. World Wildlife Fund, *Marine Turtles: Global Voyagers Threatened with Extinction*, September 2003, <http://www.worldwildlife.org/turtles/pubs/turtlebrochure.pdf> (March 31, 2008).

4. "Marine Turtles—Leatherback," *World Wildlife Fund*, n.d., <http://www.worldwildlife.org/turtles/species/lbt.cfm> (February 25, 2008).

5. World Wildlife Fund, *Conserving Marine Turtles on a Global Scale*, March 2004, <http://assets.panda.org/downloads/0304turtlereport 2nded.pdf> (September 17, 2009).

6. World Wildlife Fund, *Marine Turtles: Global Voyagers Threatened with Extinction*.

7. "How Do Marine Turtles Return to the Same Beach to Lay Their Eggs?" *ScienceDaily*, March 8, 2007, <http://www.sciencedaily.com/releases/2007/02/070226131640.htm> (April 4, 2008).

8. World Wildlife Fund, *Marine Turtles: Global Voyagers Threatened with Extinction*.

9. "Marine Turtles—Ecology," *World Wildlife Fund*, n.d., <http://www.worldwildlife.org/turtles/ecology.cfm> (February 25, 2008).

10. Ibid.

11. "Introduction—What Are the Threats," *Animals on the Edge: Marine Turtles*, n.d., <http://www.bbc.co.uk/nature/animals/conservation/turtles/> (April 4, 2008).

12. "Marine Turtles—Ecology."

13. World Wildlife Fund, *Marine Turtles: Global Voyagers Threatened with Extinction*.

14. "Marine Turtles—Ecology."

15. World Wildlife Fund, *Marine Turtles: Global Voyagers Threatened with Extinction*.

16. World Wildlife Fund, *Marine Turtles in the Wild: A WWF Species Status Report*, 2000, <http://www.wwf.or.jp/activity/wildlife/lib/marineturtles/wwfturt.pdf> (September 17, 2009).

Chapter 7. Wolves: I'll Huff and I'll Puff

1. Virginia Morell, "Wolves at the Door of a More Dangerous World," *Science*, vol. 319, February 15, 2008, p. 890.

2. Ibid.

3. "Myth and Superstition," *Wolf Country*, n.d., <www.wolfcountry.net> (November 17, 2008).

4. "Wolf Pack," *Wolf Country*, n.d., <www.wolfcountry.net> (November 17, 2008).

5. R. D. Lawrence, *In Praise of Wolves* (New York: Ballantine Books, 1986), p. 62.

6. D. J. Mladenoff, T. A. Sickley, R. G. Haight, A. P. Wydeven, "A Regional Landscape Analysis and Prediction of Favorable Gray Wolf Habitat in the Northern Great Lakes Region," *Conservation Biology*, vol. 9, no.2, April 1995, p. 280.

7. Morell, p. 892.

8. Ibid.

9. Mladenoff, Sickley, Haight, Wydeven, p. 282.

10. Ibid., p. 291.

11. Erik Zimen, "Wolf and Man: A Long History of Friendship and Enmity," n.d., <www.markings.bc.ca.mind/wolf/wolf1.html> (September 17, 2009).

12. Lawrence, p. 122.

13. Morell, p. 891.

14. J. P. Tremblay, "Ecological Impacts of Deer Overabundance on Temperate and Boreal Forests," paper presented at Society of American Foresters, June 2005, p. 54.

15. C. Carroll, M. K. Phillips, C. A. Lopez-Gonzalez, N. H. Schumaker, "Defining Recovery Goals and Strategies for Endangered Species: The Wolf as a Case Study," *BioScience*, vol. 56, no. 1, January 2006, p. 36.

Chapter 8. Sharks: Predators or Prey?

1. "Dangerous Marine Animals of Northern Australia: Sharks," *Australian Institute of Marine Science*, n.d., <http://www3.aims.gov.au/pages/research/project-net/dma/pages/sharks-02.html> (March 31, 2008).
2. "Education: Shark Finning Facts," *Sharkwater*, n.d., <http://www.sharkwater.com/education.htm> (March 31, 2008).
3. Brian Handwerk, "Shark Facts: Attack Stats, Record Swims, More," *National Geographic News*, June 13, 2005, <http://news.nationalgeographic.com/news/pf/74424729.html> (April 4, 2008).
4. "Stop Shark Finning," *The Shark Trust*, n.d., <http://www.sharktrust.org/content.asp?did=26881#what> (March 31, 2008).
5. "Sharks—The Basics," *Shark Alliance*, n.d., <http://www.sharkalliance.org/v.asp?level2id=13&rootid=13&depth=1> (March 31, 2008).
6. "Stop Shark Finning."
7. Handwerk.
8. Ibid.
9. "Stop Shark Finning."
10. "Education: Shark Finning Facts."
11. "Lines of Death: Longlining and Bycatch," *Wild Aid*, n.d., <http://www.wildaid.org/PDF/reports/Longlining_report.pdf> (March 31, 2008).
11. Ibid.
12. Ibid.
13. Peter Knights, "Sharks At Risk," *Defenders*, Winter 2002–03, pp. 13–17.
14. "Sharks at Risk," *Shark Alliance*, n.d., <http://www.sharkalliance.org/v.asp?level2id=14&rootid=14&depth=1> (March 31, 2008).
15. "Stop Shark Finning."
16. Knights.
17. "Stop Shark Finning."
18. Ibid.

Glossary

biodiversity—The presence of a wide range of different species of plants and animals in a given area.

bycatch—Animals that are caught inadvertently when another fish is the intended target.

colony collapse disorder—The phenomenon in which billions of bee colonies died suddenly for reasons that are not fully understood.

conservation—Management of a natural resource to prevent destruction or exploitation.

echolocation—The method of navigation in which bats emit pulses of high-frequency sound and use their echoes to detect obstacles.

ecosystem—All the living and nonliving things in a certain area.

endangered—At high risk of extinction in the near future.

extinct—Wiped out; the last member of the species is presumed to have died.

indicator species—Species whose sensitivity makes them ideal for showing the effect the environment is having on organisms.

keystone species—Those that affect many other living things in an ecosystem and help determine the types and numbers of other species.

polyp—A small sea animal with a tube-shaped body.

rewilding—Reintroducing once-native species into their natural landscape.

shark finning—The practice of catching a shark, cutting off the fins for sale, and discarding the animal to die in the ocean.

Further Reading

Books

Beacham, Walton, Frank V. Castronova, and Suzanne Sessine, editors. *Beacham's Guide to the Endangered Species of North America.* Detroit: Gale Group, 2001.

Gaughen, Shasta, editor. *Endangered Species.* Detroit: Greenhaven Press, 2006.

Jackson, Donna M. *The Wildlife Detectives: How Forensic Scientists Fight Crimes Against Nature.* Boston: Houghton Mifflin, 2000.

McGavin, George C. *Endangered: Wildlife on the Brink of Extinction.* Buffalo, N.Y.; Firefly Books, 2006.

Reading, Richard P., and Brian Miller. *Endangered Animals: A Reference Guide to Conflicting Issues.* Westport, Conn.: Greenwood Press, 2000.

Internet Addresses

International Union for Conservation of Nature
    <http://cms.iucn.org>

U.S. Fish and Wildlife Service: Endangered
Species Program
    <http://www.fws.gov/endangered>

World Wide Fund for Nature (World Wildlife Fund)
    <http://worldwildlife.org>

Index

A

agriculture, 13
algae, 21
almonds, 36
amphibians, 55–58
anthers, 31–34
anticoagulants, 47
antipredator mechanisms, 62
atolls, 20

B

baobab tree, 51
barrier reefs, 20
Bat Conservation International,
    54
bats
    conservation of, 50–54
    myths, 44–47
    overview, 43–44
    threats to, 47–50
bees
    conservation of, 40–42
    overview, 31
    pollination by, 31–36
    threats to, 35–40
blueberries, 36
broccoli, 36
bullfrogs, 62
bumblebees, 34, 35
bycatch, 76, 109–110

C

Canada, 16
carrots, 36
carrying capacity, 13

Children's Eternal Rain Forest,
    67
climate change effects
    coral reefs, 25, 28–29, 74–76
    frogs, 61–62
    indicators of, 25, 65
    marine turtles, 74–76
colony collapse disorder, 37, 50
conservation
    attitudes toward, 13–16
    evolution of, 10–13
    importance of, 16–17
    motivations for, 7–10, 113–
        116
coral reefs
    described, 18–21
    importance of, 21–22
    loss, impact of, 29–30
    roles of, 22–26
    threats to, 26–29, 74–76, 78
    types of, 20

D

deer, 99–101
dodo, 12

E

echolocation, 45–47
ecosystems, balance in, 6, 8–10,
    16–17
endangered species, 6, 9
Endangered Species Act, 9,
    94–96
environmental toxin effects,
    59–60. *See also* pollution
    effects.

extinction, 6, 7, 9–11

F

fringing reefs, 20
frogs
    conservation of, 67, 68
    loss, impacts of, 64–68
    overview, 55–58
    threats to, 58–64

G

genetic material, loss of, 10
Global Amphibian Assessment,
    59, 65–68
global warming. *See* climate
    change effects.

H

habitat loss effects
    bats, 52
    bees, 37, 39, 40
    coral reefs, 74
    frogs, 58–59
    generally, 11, 16
    marine turtles, 73–74
    wolves, 84–86, 95, 98
harlequin frogs, 60–61
honey, 33
honeybees, 34, 39
human activity effects
    bat colony disturbance,
        49–50
    coral reefs, 27–29
    marine turtles, 76
    overview, 11–13
    wolves, 84–86, 94–98
humans as stewards, 8, 17

I

International Union for
    Conservation of Nature and
    Natural Resources (IUCN),
    7, 9, 65

K

Kemp's Ridley turtles, 71, 72

L

Land Reserves Period, 15
leatherback turtles, 71

M

marine turtles
    conservation of, 80–81
    life cycle, 70–73
    loss, impacts of, 78–80
    overview, 69–70
    threats to, 73–78
misunderstandings, 5
Monteverde Cloud Forest
    Preserve, 60–61, 67

N

National Marine Fisheries
    Service, 9
natural selection, 11
Nature and Wilderness
    Reserves Period, 15

O

onions, 36
oranges, 36
Organisation for Economic
    Cooperation and
    Development, 7
overfishing, 28–29, 110–112

P

Pacific Island cultures, 23, 30
pandas, 6
passenger pigeon, 12
pesticide effects
    bats, 54
    bees, 37, 39, 40
    frogs, 59–60, 65
plant reproduction, 31–34
platform reefs, 20
pollination, 31–36, 50–51
pollution effects, 26, 76–77
predation effects, 62–63, 77–78

R

rabies, 45
Recreation Reserves Period, 15
Resource Reserve Period, 15
Roosevelt, Theodore, 16

S

sea grass beds, 74, 78–80
sharks
    attacks by, 104–105
    conservation of, 112
    finning, 107–109
    long-lining, 109–110
    loss, impacts of, 105–107
    overfishing, 110–112
    overview, 69
stigmas, 31–34
sweet cherries, 36
symbiosis, 21

T

threats
    to bats, 47–50
    to bees, 35–40
    to coral reefs, 26–29, 74–76,
        78
    to frogs, 58–64
    by humans. *See* human
        activity effects
    to marine turtles, 73–78
    to wolves, 94–98
tourism
    coral reefs, 22, 24–25
    marine turtles, 80
    pollution effects, 26
Tree Reserves Period, 15
turtles. *See* marine turtles.

U

ultraviolet radiation, 61–62
U.S. Fish and Wildlife Service,
    9, 85–86, 96

V

vampire bats, 47

W

wolves
    behaviors, 86–94
    conservation of, 101–103
    human activity effects,
        84–86, 94–98
    loss, impacts of, 98–101
    overview, 82–84
    threats to, 94–98